Reading is Walking
The Encyclopedia Series

©Gonçalo M. Tavares, 2006 (for: *Breves Notas sobre a Ciência*),
©Gonçalo M. Tavares, 2007 (for: *Breves Notas sobre o Medo*)
©Gonçalo M. Tavares, 2009 (for: *Breves Notas sobre as Ligações*)
©Gonçalo M. Tavares, 2015 (for: *Breves Notas sobre a Música*)
©Gonçalo M.Tavares, 2019 (for: *Breves Notas sobre Literatura-Bloom*).

By arrangement with *Literarische Agentur Mertin Inh.
Nicole Witt e.K.*, Frankfurt am Main, Germany.

©Quantum Prose, Inc. 2019, for this edition:
Reading is Walking: The Encyclopedia Series

Editorial Director
Marta del Pozo

Proofreaders
Gregg Harper & James Steele

Designer
Vicente Sánchez

Author's Photography
©Joanna Caiano

Cover photography
@Orproject
Title: Umami Series; Project Architect: Rajat Sodhi; Project Team: Sambit Samant; Client: Art d'Inox; Manufacturer: Rachaita Creative Solutions; Photographs: Sumedh Prasad.
Orproject has used its research into anisotropic material aggregations to develop the geometries, which form networks, surfaces and volumes based on single curved metal sheets. Digitally calculated as material deformations of force-based vector fields, the morphologies create dense and open distributions of the steel strips that distort and form curved volumes.

ISBN: 978-0-9973014-2-7

Library of Congress Control Number: 2018953231

Quantum Prose, Inc.
New York, NY

www.quantumprose.org

Reading is Walking
The Encyclopedia Series

Gonçalo M. Tavares

Translation and Foreword by
Rhett McNeil

QUANTUM PROSE

Contents

The Notecards of Translator McNeil   ix

Brief Notes on Science   19

Brief Notes on Fear   155

Brief Notes on Connections
(Llansol, Molder and Zambrano)   214

Brief Notes on Music   281

Brief Notes on Bloom-Literature   375

THE NOTECARDS OF TRANSLATOR MCNEIL

NOTECARD 1

Gonçalo M. Tavares has, as of the writing of this essay, published 40? books, all of them marked on the final page with the phrase "Notebooks of Gonçalo M. Tavares" and the number that corresponds to the volume at hand.

NOTECARD 2

Many of these books are parts of a series of books. These series bear names like: Encyclopedia, Classical Studies, The Kingdom, The Neighborhood, Investigations, Cities, and so on.

NC 3

The books in the omnibus volume that follows in my translation from the Portuguese make up the complete (at this moment) *Encyclopedia Series*, and are numbers 19, 22, 26, 37, and 39 in the Notebooks of Gonçalo M. Tavares.

NC 4

These books in the present volume are not exactly encyclopedias; perhaps they are nothing like encyclopedias. Or maybe they are encyclopedic in their attempts to approach a given subject (let's say Fear, Music…) from as many novel viewpoints as possible. They are possibly encyclopedias of poetic approaches to a specific subject matter.

NC 5

What one can say for certain of these and other works by Tavares is very little, since they shift and alter their aesthetic and philosophical aims from one sentence to the next, one paragraph to the next, one page to the next.

NC 6

Yet perhaps not from one volume to the next. There is an unmistakable narrative voice, or poetic voice, or literary style, or aesthetic project, or epistemological refusal common to all of the Notebooks of Gonçalo M. Tavares.

NC 7

This will be fertile territory for a would-be critic or scholar of the Notebooks: How does Tavares create a formally and tonally homogenous body of work when his aesthetic principles and narrative/poetic aims seem to be so temporary as to change at times in the middle of a sentence?

NC 8

The final book in the volume in your hand at this moment, *Brief Notes on Bloom Literature*, provides some insight into Tavares's body of work as a whole, even though it purports to be an investigation into what he calls "Bloom-Literature."

NC 9

He indicates in the prefatory material to this book that only one, maybe two, of his books might be classified as "Bloom-Literature," and even then maybe not every part of them, and also perhaps not even the volume at hand, the *Brief Notes on Bloom Literature*.

NC 10

It is a paradoxical manifesto, in that it negates its own principles and makes them provisional and not always applicable. A provisional manifesto, a suspect manifesto in dictionary form, brief notes on an aesthetic approach that no one, not even Tavares, nor his Translator McNeil, abides by in its entirety, or even often.

NC 11

This is telling. The work is its own twisting, shifting, sometimes opaque self. It is beyond dictums of good writing or calls for experimental forms. It experiments constantly, a perpetual revolution in form, unafraid of shocking the reader with abrupt changes and sentences that refuse to take the correct turn at the crossroads. Indeed, one could categorize his entire approach to writing as:

NC 12

*This notecard is missing. An enterprising young editor, whom I shall call Klaus, absconded with this notecard and certain other of my translations of and musings on Gonçalo M. Tavares, including other notecards (this is how I organize my thoughts, I carry them around and put them in and out of order) on which I had written about Tavares and José Saramago, Tavares and Enrique Vila-Matas, Tavares and Camões, Tavares and María Gabriela Llansol. These notecards, along with two packages of herring crisps, a postcard written—though not delivered—to an old lover in Potsdam, a pair of collectible beer bottlecaps from the early days of brewing in Qingdao (rare and expensive beer bottlecaps having long been my preferred method of taking large sums of money across international borders without having to give an explanation or pay a duty or a bribe), a handwritten invitation to a weekend-long party and séance at the house of a reclusive intaglio printmaker in Batumi (an acquaintance from Tbilisi showed me a number of photographs she clandestinely took at this party, which not only show Klaus in attendance, but also show him disguised as me, and seemingly, in a slightly blurry image, showing others the aforementioned postcard and gleefully laughing at it), and, most importantly, a passport from a country that is not my own, which took years of careful planning and artful forgery to acquire, were all brazenly stolen by the editor Klaus. If this prologue is lacking, if I am now unable to travel freely, if five years' worth of translator's fees in the form of two bottlecaps have likely been mistaken for rubbish or worthless parts of an obsessive's collection, we all have Klaus to blame.

NC 13

An artist's rendering. A text rendered in English. A rendering plant. A rendering of a plant. A plant. An informer.

NC 14

Someone said: "A translation is a baseball rolled across a room to a person on the other side. It rolls nearer and nearer the player, so close they can see the stitches on the ball. It never fully arrives. Sometimes it transforms into a crystal ball on its way. Sometimes it gathers moss."

NC 15

The vocabulary used by Tavares in these and other of his books is deceptively simple. The syntax less so. The ideas often byzantine. The approaches to poetic, narrative, and philosophical problems, baroque.

NC 16

Many a translator delights at the search for an unknown word, a regionalism, a neologism, a long-forgotten children's sing-song rhyme that accompanies an equally forgotten game of marbles or hopscotch. Tavares's books afford none of these pleasures.

NC 17

Instead, the translator must sweat the syntax, make the language jar and cage-rattle just as Tavares's language does in the original.

NC 18

Those rare or obscure words, once discovered by a diligent translator, would likely get rendered into the target language in a similar or identical manner by many different translators.

NC 19

The stumble-steady sentence, the clause crinkled back upon itself: these may have as many equivalents in English as there are willing translators.

NC 20

This is a relief to a translator. Which is its own form of worry.

NC 21

*This notecard has been replaced by a stone. I did this to indicate something about the translation process but can no longer recall what it was meant to signify. It is now just a stone.

NC 22

I think these books owe something to Kafka's aphorisms.

NC 23

Someone said: "A translation is a boat that carries readers to an ostensible destination where it cannot dock. Some boats offer scenic coastal cruising with a tour guide's commentary piped through speakers on all decks, maniacally loud— passengers cover their ears, become seasick. Some boats get dashed, spectacularly so, against rocks far from the destination, to the passengers' inexplicable delight."

NC 24

Someone said: "There are other outcomes as well."

NC 25

What are these books? We've established that they are not encyclopedias in the traditional sense. The last volume looks like an idiosyncratic dictionary. The first four are poetic meditations on a subject. Philosophical poetry. Or the other way around.

NC 26

Tavares's 27th Notebook is entitled *Brief Notes on Connections (Llansol, Molder, and Zambrano)*. It is quite distinct from the first three volumes (notes on Science, Fear, and Music), in that it is not about "connections" writ large (whatever that would be), but connections between Tavares and three other authors, all named María (or Maria). More specifically, *Connections* is the creation of connective textual tissue between this 27th book and passages from works by the three Marías/Marias.

NC 27

The title of this volume comes from *Brief Notes on Connections*, Tavares by way of Llansol, who writes: "In terms of movement, I went to Sintra, I read Hölderlin."

NC 28

To which Tavares replies: "There is, in this back and forth movement of the legs of a person who is immobile and reading, an impressive march, *a traversing*: Reading is Walking."

NC 29

I misspoke in Notecard 28. I meant to say "Translator McNeil by way of editor del Pozo by way of Tavares by way of Llansol, who writes of Hölderlin." A fine traversing.

NC 30

A traversing. A boat ride on the rolling sea. The ball keeps rolling. Let's get the ball rolling.

NC 31

Snippets from Saramago on Tavares: "there is very much a before Gonçalo M. Tavares and an after," "in thirty years' time, if not before, Tavares will win the Nobel Prize," "Tavares burst onto the Portuguese literary scene armed with an utterly original imagination," "combined with a language entirely his own." "One feels like punching him."

NC 32

Someone said: "Who writes the translated text? Who is the author? It is not a tangible someone with a passport and a fingerprint. It is the ineffable 'someone' of the phrase 'someone said . . .'. So it is neither Homer nor Pope, neither Pushkin nor Nabokov . . . it is Someone."

NC 33

I disagree with what Someone said in Notecard 32. Gonçalo M. Tavares wrote the books in this present volume. Every word of them, I swear. No trickery or hoaxes here.

NC 34

*This notecard was nibbled by a small domesticated animal, torn to tiny tatters. Illegible.

NC 35

Enough, then, from me. I hereby roll the baseball to your side of the room. It may transform into a crystal ball. It may gather moss.

Brief Notes on Science

Dedicated to António Franco Alexandre

We have seen how it is originally language which works on the construction of concepts, a labor taken over in later ages by science.

Nietzsche

Danger

It is clear that Danger is the origin of the most efficient scientific methods.

If Man were immortal, he would not yet have invented the wheel (one could say).

Tedium and Conclusions

It's tedium. Or else, the other element. Jorge Luis Borges affirmed that a literary text is only considered finished and definitive for two classes of reasons: weariness or religious faith. Thus too in scientific experiments.

Abstraction

Abstraction is useful in science if, as in the children's tale, you leave a trail of breadcrumbs in order to identify the way back. However, sometimes you are the one who, absentmindedly or out of hunger, devours the very possibility of return. And you remain there, lost: among the splendid ideas.

(The more you walk, the more your appetite grows, and your path becomes circular. If you're hungry and spot a breadcrumb in front of you, what do you do?

This is the scientist lost in the forest.)

Differences and Similarities (1)

Spotting the differences is one of the methods. Spotting the similarities is another.

The mosquito that disturbs your harmony of sound and space, when it is smashed between your swift hands, becomes silent—just like your hands after the action. Thereafter you throw the mosquito out, and the harmony of sound and space returns. But don't imagine that it is definitive, this harmony. You know very well that it is not.

Differences and Similarities (2)

We can kill the mosquito or point at it and say: Mosquito. Classifications and categories begin with disharmony.

Differences and Similarities (3)

And harmony begins with Cruelty.
"At a certain altitude, all is one," wrote Nietzsche in *The Philosopher's Book*.

Precision

To be precise in science is to make a mistake in a tone of voice that is more forceful than that of others.

To put it another way: you pick up the target with both hands and press the bull's-eye against point of the arrowhead.

This is scientific precision.

Feelings and Science

What is science useful for if it does not investigate feelings?
It is useful for that which is not feeling.
Is it, therefore, useful for man?
It is useful for every part of man that is not feeling.

The Familiar

Science does not proceed toward Mystery. Nor toward the Strange.
Science proceeds toward the Familiar.

Investigating (1)

How would it be possible to proceed toward Mystery? Toward that which I do not know?

If I proceed towards Mystery it is because the Mystery has already been solved by me.

If such a thing were to happen at the circus, people would call it a farce.

You already know where they hid the jewel (you were the one who hid it) and now you're asking them to put a blindfold over your eyes.

What are you doing, they ask you.

Investigating, you reply.

Investigating (2)

But you're not investigating: you're entertaining yourself.

You invent difficulties and concepts in order to delay your arrival.

Tomorrow you shall arrive at the hiding place where just yesterday you hid the answer.

Drawing and Science

Everything that you cannot draw is an abstraction. Everything that you cannot draw is useless.
(But how does one draw these two sentences?
Is it useless to say that almost everything is useless? This is a problem.)

Anthropomorphism

It is clear that science is anthropomorphic.

Is there anything that a serpent does that one could say is not the action of a serpent?

All the acts of man are acts of man. (And science is an act of Man.)

It is as large as the way we want to see it, and it is as small as the way we want to see it.

(If you have a certain type of mirror you shall see, when facing it, an enormous image, but if you change your position and the position and characteristics of the mirror, you can see, when facing it, how small you are.

It is clear that your size isn't conferred by you, but by the tape measure. But you were the one who invented the tape measure.)

Hatred, Love, and Science

You can do science out of hatred for a cause or a group of people.

You can do science out of love for a cause or a group of people.

You can obtain, out of hatred or love, identical scientific conclusions.

Lies and Truth

It is the organism—and its systems of repulsion and attraction—that decides if something is true or false.

A Lie is that which repels my organic system of Truth detection.

To say, then, that a lie is a lie seems like an overstatement.

History of the Sciences (1)

The History of the Sciences always finds itself slightly delayed in relation to the History of Desires.

There are some famous metaphors, let's make use of them.

It is as if the horses were Desire and the cart that's pulled by them was Science.

If the horses were detached from the cart, they would gain speed, but would lose their public utility; society wants functions, not flight.

But the worst happens with the cart itself. If the horses are detached from it, it will never move again.

History of the Sciences (2)

It is clear that it is the scientist with his whip who steers the horses and the cart.

History of the Sciences (3)

If we enter into psychoanalytic territory we could say that childhood, pleasures, and fears guide the scientist's whip.

History of the Sciences (4)

If we enter into mystical terrain we could say that it is Destiny that guides the childhood, pleasures, and fears of an individual.

History of the Sciences (5)

Scientific investigations depend, therefore, on God, Chance, or Destiny (or whatever you want to call it).
But, despite all this, they also depend on Reason.

The Theory of Snow

We know what snow is. It's enchanting, today. We play with it. We look around us and all we see is its white color. Our world has been taken over by the snow.

We know, therefore, what snow is. And we know what a scientific theory is.

It's just that Winter is not eternal.

Coercion and the Ephemeral (1)

Let's talk about an illusion.

It is not the coercive force of things on the investigator that imposes the temporary truth of science.

It is, rather, the coercive force of the investigator on the things that imposes the temporary truth of science.

Coercion and the Ephemeral (2)

Because it is easy to see: it isn't the things that are temporary, it's the investigators who are temporary.

Newton died, as is well known; but the things that he saw did not.

(And the things that he saw, and their transformations, are now called by other names by the living.)

Validation and Generations

Those who are now living determine what the Truth is.
It is the living generation that validates science.
It is clear that it wasn't Einstein who proved that the theory of Relativity was true. It is the current generation that proves it when it declares that the proof that Einstein presented was correct.
In terms of the validation of Truth, the most significant dead scientists are less important than the least significant living scientist.
It's a narrative question: you know the end (the present) of the film. They died halfway through it.

The Minimal and the Large

To minimal things, science adds large things.
To large things, science adds small things.

Skepticism and Belief

Skeptical like the skeptics, believing like the believers.

The half that advances is the believer, the half that confirms is the skeptic.

But the perfect scientist is also a gardener: he believes that beauty is knowledge.

(The beautiful person holds a secret. She has discovered something.)

Beauty and Science

Beautification is another scientific methodology. Beauty is one of the shouts of Eureka.

Investigations and Disequilibrium

Lean forward into the future: at one end only your feet remain on the ground, your head presses forward.
Investigating without disequilibrium is trudging through mud: someone is going to sink.

The New and Specialists

You can only add something to World 1—whether it be a scientific discipline or merely an idea—if you have brought something from World 2.

To put it another way, and this being the obvious way forward:

Nothing that belongs to World 1 is new to World 1.

You want to bring yourself something new? Get outside yourself.

You want to bring something new to this cubic box that measures 1 meter by 1 meter?

Then search for something outside of it.

This is the obvious presupposition of any investigation.

How, then, are we to understand specialists?

The Quotidian

The profound consequences of science can be observed in the habits of a housewife, a six year-old child, or a dying old man.

Observe the habits of a society and you shall see the extraordinary plane at which it has arrived.

In a thunderstorm light comes first, and only much later does sound arrive.

The River

What fraction of knowledge is enough for me to be happy?
What fraction of knowledge is enough for me to make others happy?
Is that which science discovers outside of these two fractions the part that is useless?
(And on which bank of the river do you find yourself?)

Classification

Classification is unanimous poetry.
(Useless, therefore, for an individual.)

Language

Language utilizes science to achieve the illusion of Truth, just as language utilizes art to achieve the illusion of a certain sort of Beauty.

The Stupid

The only way to think—which is to say, to move forward—is to be imprecise, inexact, in relation to that which has already been thought.

Whoever, in a debate, accuses the other, saying:

"This is one more alteration in relation to what Your Excellence has said previously."

Whoever says this is, in fact, accusing themselves.

Imitation

If what is now being thought is identical to what has already been thought, then such is not thought, it is imitation.
"You're not thinking, you're imitating."
This is a nasty insult.

Objects

Whoever defends the objectivity of science effaces herself as a subject and takes pride in this—she considers it an indispensable part of the method.

However, there are people who do not believe in a science that is made up of objects.

The Cup

An object does not investigate anything.
A cup, for example; either they put water in it or wine or some other liquid, or they drop it on the floor.

Scientific Instruments

Scientific instruments aren't a response in Form to the Function of the Mysteries of the World.

Each scientific instrument is a response to the necessities of an investigator.

Instruments and Mystery

The investigator's Hammer doesn't hammer the nails of the Mystery of the World, it hammers the nails of the investigator's own mind.
(And those of his heart as well.)

Boredom

Is an unhappy scientific investigator a good scientific investigator?
Is a lovesick scientific investigator a good scientific investigator?
Those are two different problems, says the bored man.
And this one, indeed, the bored man, cannot be a good investigator.

Joy and Sadness

But persist.
What is the relationship between happiness and scientific method?
Are there happy scientific methodologies?
Are there sad scientific methodologies?
I dare say that there are.

A Hypothesis

Joy is a catalyst for a scientific experiment; sadness, an inhibitor.
Sadness restricts; how can a sad man discover something?
Only those who are happy take risks.
Sadness is anti-scientific.

Your Excellence

"Your Excellence is not utilizing the scientific method appropriately."
Because Your Excellence is sad.

The Evidence of the Proof

For joy, everything is evident, everything is clear, everything is proven.

Not so for sadness.

Joy is indispensable in science because the illusion of evidence, which only joy can arrive at, is also indispensable.

Proving something, proving anything at all, is an exuberance of the joyful heart.

"You believe in yourself to such an extent that you believe in that which your mind proves."

Love

The useful methodology is a hammer.
Science uses the hammer.
Art uses science.
(And love can render everything useless.)

Love of Facts

Let's return to the question at hand.

Can a lovesick man prove something? Should we believe in him, in his objectivity (as it is called)?

And can a man who is not lovesick prove something?

But there is another way to approach the topic: understanding love as a way to prove something.

"For me, this fact is more than proven: I love this fact."

The Manner of Arriving at Things

Wittgenstein on methodology and the thing in itself:
"So—you say—*what* is judged here is independent of the method of judging it. What length *is* cannot be defined by the method of determining length.—To think this is to make a mistake. What mistake?—To say: 'The height of Mont Blanc depends on how one climbs it' would be queer."

I can investigate the thing or the way of arriving at the thing.

Error

I don't make these sorts of errors. I make those sorts of errors.

(Not making an error on one side is to make an error on the other. Because there is a balance between things. There are things on two sides.)

If you didn't fail here, find out where you did fail, because there is no such thing as not failing; there is only looking at the place where you didn't fail.

Look, therefore, at the other place. The one you have your back to.

The Look

Your problem is not the Problem.
Your problem is the part of the Problem that you're not looking at.

The Look, Once More

Or even at the Solution.
Your solution is the part of the Solution that you are looking at.

Eyes

Only by looking at all sides at once will you be able to see the Problem, which is to say: the Solution.
In this way, you see nothing.
Or better put: you see what your eyes want to see. Which is to say: you see your eyes.

To Arrive at the Beginning: Methodology

You don't use a methodology. You are the methodology that you use.

(Or: you don't arrive at a result. You arrive at a methodology.

Or even: you don't prove a fact or a theory, you prove a methodology.)

Difficulty

Which is to say: when you exclaim at some point in your investigation: "I have arrived at the end!" you should exclaim: "I have arrived at the beginning!"

(And it's not out of ostensible humility that you should say this, on the contrary: it's out of ostensible ego. I have arrived at myself—this is what you should exclaim—and how difficult it is to arrive at myself!)

The Change in Identity of the Investigator

When you don't obtain results, you decide to change Identity.

If you remain the same, how can you achieve something different?

(It is one's fingers that feel and touch something. And not the other way around.)

The Second Mathematics

Wittgenstein's question:
"If all men believed that 2 x 2 = 5, would 2 x 2 still equal 4?"

There exists a second Mathematics behind the first. It is made up of that which is Error in the first, and yet is still—like the first Mathematics—made up of order and rules. The errors of the second Mathematics are also indisputable propositions in the first Mathematics.

(Thinking about opposites. About evil and goodness. About exactitude and error. About the high and the low.)

Regulation of Error

If we habituate ourselves to Error, if we elaborate a regulation of Error—rules by which Error never fails, or rather: rules in order to avoid the act of getting it right—if we habituate ourselves to such a thing, we will be able, in time, to make the act of getting it right illegal.
Laws come from habits, not from Truth.

Thinking Twice

Observing one's own thought is to think on top of one's initial thinking. It isn't as easy as looking at your own feet while you walk.

The most important thought is the one that emerges as the final observation.

Experiment and Sensations

Can you perform experiments with your sensations in the same way that you perform experiments with chemical substances?

All experiments are doubles (at least): you perform an experiment with chemical substances, experimenting on this experiment with your sensations.

Performing experiments directly with your sensations is, therefore, to reduce the distance between you and reality by half.

Falsifications

How do you falsify the false?
By making it true, this is the obvious response.
But if we think about it a little, we will realize that we stand before a lengthy paradox. Something that could paralyze us.

Multiplication of the Truth

The true is a falsification of the false.
And there isn't just one falsification of the false, there are many. Such are truths, and such are lies.

The Present

Today's useful connection is the one that resolves yesterday's problems.

The Tone of Voice

Can the tone of voice in which a scientific theory is presented influence the effects of this theory on the World? The response is: yes.

Evidence and Strength

The evident is that which is stronger than we are.

Take note, this has nothing to do with truth or lie, with the proven or unproven, it has to do with strength and weakness.

If you replace the expression
"This is evident!"
with:
"This is strong!"
you will better capture the meaning of the first expression.

Scientific evidence persists only while that which surrounds it is weak.

Proof and Power

Proof is a question of power, not of veracity.
(As in classical warfare: the greatness of the generals and the number of soldiers gives the army its power.)

The Center of the Eye and the Corner of the Eye

To observe out of the corner of the eye is, in science, to begin to elaborate a hypothesis.

That which is observed by the center of the eye is the evident, the obvious, that which is shared by the masses.

In science, as in the world of inventions, to observe out of the corner of the eye is to see a different detail, one that is the beginning of anything of significance.

To observe reality out of the corner of the eye, that is to say: to think slightly to the side. This is what is called creativity. All important scientific theories have come out of this.

Scientific Community

The scientific community looks out of the center of the eye.
The great investigators look out of the corner of the eye.

Scientific Proof

Scientific proof is a kind of centering of the eye.
After something is proven, that which was looked at out of the corner of the eye is now looked at out of the center of the eye.

New Theory

A new theory repositions the detail (or even the insignificant), turning it into the center.

All that is small can be positioned in such a way that, to our eyes, it seems large. Recall the brutal experiment in which your finger is larger than a skyscraper.

Followers

However, your finger is not, to others, larger than a skyscraper.

It would only be such if others placed themselves directly behind your finger.

(As followers of a theory do.)

Errors of One or of Many

Scientific errors are the errors of a scientific community. The error of One (without followers) is what we call Art.

Science and Democracy

Science is a democracy in which each person counts as a vote. But it isn't the entire population that votes, it's only the scientists, the investigators.

In this manner, to make this all clearer, the same way that political parties present themselves at elections, scientific theories should present themselves to scientists. And they are the ones who vote.

The victorious theory, as is the case in this day and age, would be called Truth.

This is how something is proven in science.

Collective Poetry

Is poetry not science?
Poetry is individual science.
Collective poetry is useful: this is scientific theory.

Love and the Object of Study

The gaze of someone who loves upon the object of their love is identical to the gaze of the scientist upon the object of their study.
To pay attention to the thing we love, we cannot pay attention to the things around it (beyond a certain radius, taking the beloved person as the center of the circumference). The same occurs in scientific studies.
To say that the gaze of the lover is the true gaze is folly. But no one says this.
To say that the gaze of the specialist is the true gaze is also folly. But in this case there are many who say this.
If the truth is a circumference (let's do this geometric exercise), it will certainly not have a limited radius. However, every gaze—be it that of the lover upon the beloved or that of the scientist upon the object of study—has, obligatorily, a limited radius. Everything found beyond that radius does not receive the attention of the gaze.
As such, sometimes the distracted (or non-obsessed) gaze is the one that captures the most important things.
Only a person who isn't enamored of A can see that, to the side of A, B is to be found.
And B could be the most beautiful, the most true; could make you happier.

Theory and Society

We consider true the scientific theory that makes us happiest individually (or that makes us the least unhappy). Truth is a selfish decision.

The Lie of Things

Can the reality of phenomena dissemble the same way that we feign fear when we aren't afraid? Could it be that what we call truth is nothing more than a simulation that arises from Reality?

Why is it that we attribute the capacity to lie exclusively to humans?

Can an atom lie? Can a chemical substance lie? A stone?

All our science agrees upon the presupposition that reality does not lie.

It's an unproved presupposition.

And what if reality lies to us? Is it dissembling? Is it dramatizing?

If I don't want to worry the person I love, I pretend that I have no sorrows, when, in fact, I have many sorrows.

Or: if I want to scare someone I don't like, I pretend to be afraid when I'm not afraid at all.

We always think that the capacity to lie or consciously conceal is associated with affect. We always think that the things that surround us have no affect [ok, some animals do: dogs can dissemble, cats, lions. But, for example: is it possible for us to think of a virus that dissembles? Of a virus that lies? If so (some illnesses and treatments perhaps confirm this), then what about an atom? No? A planet? Could a planet have the capacity to lie? To hide something the way we hide the sorrow we feel?].It's as if you are drawing a borderline, from which you say: anything smaller than this cannot lie, and anything larger than this also cannot lie.

In fact, you have drawn the proportions and defined the type of organism that you accept as having the capacity to lie or dissemble. And all other proportions and existences are, for you, incapable of lying and, therefore, completely true.

But why place that borderline right there? Why not somewhere else?

Let me respond to this: about that which you do not know well, you say: this cannot lie to me (the stone, the atom, the planet). But this is absurd. Apply this rule to people, for example. Are you certain that those people you don't know are not liars? You know a dog and say of it: sometimes it pretends that it's really cold, but in truth it wants something else entirely.

Is it difficult to think this way about a planet or an atom?

Do things really not want anything from us?

Do things not have a justification for lying to us?

We shouldn't be so naïve. The survival instinct and the instinct to seek happiness are shared by the universe of things. And these two instincts make us, from time to time, tell the truth or do the truthful thing, and, at other times, tell a lie or do something untruthful.

Error and Lie

Sometimes, then, the scientist's Error should be called Reality's Lie.

Lie Detection

Science should be understood as the search for the *truth realized by things*. Science as a methodology that aims to detect the simulations and lies of reality and to bring what is true within it to the surface.
"Look, I proved that reality is lying to us *right there*."

True and False

Replace the expression:
"This is true"
with the expression:
"This is the truth of this thing."
It isn't your theory that is true; your theory detected the truth of a phenomenon (at least this is what you believe).
Nothing is true or false. Everything exists and sometimes dissembles or lies. At other times it doesn't.
"This is true and false. And the part of this that is true is this part."
(And thus you have your scientific theory at hand.)

Lies

A new theory is not, and should not be, the discovery of what is untrue in what has been written about a given phenomenon. On the contrary, it is the discovery of what is untrue about the phenomenon itself.

It isn't pointing a finger at the scientists who developed the old theory and saying:

"You were wrong."

It's pointing a finger at the object of study and saying:

"You lied to them."

There Are No Errors

To assert: there are no Errors in science, there are lies that reality presents.

The Fatigue of Things Observed

There are things that don't dissemble, you say. A newborn baby doesn't know how to *come up* with lies.

Very well, that's exactly right: you have to look at the object of study when it is newly born.

(And don't forget that throughout our lives we all have periods or moments in which we are newborns. It is at these moments that, if someone were to look at us, they would see our truth.)

Thus the importance of long periods of observation, for only when the object of study is tired is it true. Your gaze must remained fixed upon the object until it is tired. (Fatigue as a sudden appearance; like a thing that is newly born.) The problem is that your gaze is almost always the thing that tires first.

Discovery of Lies

Who is the first to become fatigued: your observant gaze or the observed phenomenon?

Arriving, or not, at the truth of a phenomenon depends on this.

Truth is arrived at through a resistance to fatigue on the part of the observer. Lies are arrived at through the fatigue of the observer. When the observer finds herself tired of waiting, she exclaims: I made a discovery!; and ends her investigation.

I have discovered a lie, she should say.

Prolonged Methodology

But the discovery of lies is one stage of science. It is a methodology.

If you were to be exhaustive in this methodology, which is to say, if you were to discover all the lies of a given thing, then you would have discovered the truth of that thing (which is all that's left).

But this is a prolonged process.

Direct Revelations of the True

But this is the only process that science utilizes: discover the successive lies of a given thing. The methods that remain are direct revelations of the true, and here we cannot speak of science, but of religion. Or of chance.

Slowness

Science is slow because phenomena lie a lot.

Truth and Drawings

Is it truer to draw the true or to write it?

This might seem like a ridiculous question, but the fact is that science considers the writing of the true to be the truest.

Another question: is it possible to write that which is true about a phenomenon and impossible to draw it or photograph it?

Could it be that a good painter is incapable of painting the truth?

Could it be that letters, the alphabet, are closer to truth—could it be that they are truer than brush strokes, pen strokes, and color?

[And the strangest thing about all this is that there is an infinitude of languages (an infinitude of associations of letters towards the truth of a given thing), whereas if you draw a human body, everyone will understand it.]

There is something strange, we could even say: there is something mystical about the conviction that the word better describes the truth of the world (or that it approximates it more).

The Failure of Men

Let me say this: if you had believed more in drawing than in writing, you would be closer to what is true in the World.

It was a question of beliefs, a wager on a horse race.

Men bet on the wrong horse. This is a possible summary of the history of the sciences (and not the only one). Why don't there exist different languages of drawing? Drawings in different languages?

Inventions and Truth

There are no incorrect concepts.

Each concept is an invention of language, an attempt to approximate the language of things.

There are no incorrect inventions.

There are no false inventions, just as there are no false concepts.

True and false are categories that are not applicable to concepts. Useful and useless, yes. Accepted by many and accepted by few, yes.

All inventions are true (don't forget this).

Truth and Beauty

Truth is Beauty repeated. Or: the true is foreseeable Beauty (we know that at that moment, at that place, a given thing will appear).

Science and Selfishness

To solve problems that are not a cause of unhappiness is to play a game of solitaire, solitary and selfish. But solving problems is always a cause of happiness.

Laws of Illogic

Language possesses what thought possesses, and language and thought possess what the world possesses: logic and illogic, metaphor and redundancy.

If I am capable of saying/writing the illogic (dream and madness), it is because I am capable of thinking it, and if I think it, it's because it exists.

Of course science wants to go deeper. But to know and go deeper into what? I reply: to know and go deeper into logic—that which can be structured by laws.

As for knowing and going deeper into illogic, which has no rules, science flees from such a wolf. When science approaches it, it does so in order to project (with a light) laws towards that which never repeats.

The Unrepeatable and Science

Science studies that which repeats. It retreats from the unique or makes that which is unique into a soldier: as if the unrepeatable were merely a detail of something Larger, which ultimately repeats.

Science says: if it is unrepeatable, if it has no laws, if it isn't foreseeable, if it is, then, illogical, then it is just a detail. The most important thing, for science, is that which repeats, this seems obvious. However, any child knows that a quantity of 1 makes any good precious.

Science, some immoderate critics will say, isn't interested in the diamond, which is rare; science is fascinated with pebbles, which are plentiful.

The Two Objects of Study

Science prohibits lies, yet lies exist, and everything that exists is true.
The object of science is Truth, but in this science forgets the 2nd part of the World, the 2nd part of reality: the lie.
Science should have 2 objects of study: the truth of things and the lie of things.

Object and Objective of Study

Do not confuse the object of study with the objective of study.

We can accept that the objective of science is the truth of things, however science starts from the presupposition that its object of study is still the truth of things.

This posits, then, the following question: how can I arrive at truth by studying a lie?

In fact, what happened was this: science put this very question to itself and concluded: only by studying the truth can I arrive at the truth. And from then on, any time someone contests their object of study, scientists puff with pride and proclaim: we study truth.

Investigations and Hypotheses of Truth

But no. You study truth just as much as lies. You study this object precisely because you do not know if it (or what you think about it) is truth or lie.

If your science is good, you will arrive at truth from the starting point of your object of study (which can be true or not). To claim more than this is to claim too much.

If your object of study is Truth, why are you studying?

One does not investigate Truth, one investigates hypotheses of truth.

The Lie as Raw Material

The lie is an object of scientific study.
If the lie did not exist, investigations would not exist.

To Exist or Not Exist

Science despises paradoxes and contradictions. But science arises (or should arise) in order to resolve paradoxes and contradictions.

Sensation as Method

You have other instruments—your sensations. And everything emerges from them.

They are your map. Nevertheless, there are infinite possibilities of scale; and before you start running, you must confirm that the map is really of the place in which you are lost.

Are Sensations True?

The question is this: if your problem is the place in which you are lost, and the map—your sensations, your mode of perception—is the only way to locate yourself (to resolve the problem), then how arrogant an illusion is this illusion—to think that you have in your hand the right map for that area?

And what if you have the wrong map?

(Or rather: and what if the capacity of your sensations is not enough even to perceive the problem?)

Effort and Flight

Science always starts from the principle that it has the right map. And thus it thinks that it's only a matter of searching.

It supposes that effort and sweat will suffice.

(And, ultimately, they should often be flying instead of excavating—which is physically impossible for them.)

Metaphors

The metaphor, being an instrument of non-logical language, can touch, which is to say explain (or prove) things that logical language can neither touch nor explain.

They are two tools: logical language and metaphors. With a hammer, you drive nails. With a handsaw, you cut wood.

(If you observed a carpenter trying to solve all his problems with a hammer, you would say: He's crazy!

Or at most you would try to help him, pointing toward the other instruments: look at the handsaw over there, it's the ideal tool for sawing wood. Don't do it with the hammer, you'll ruin everything and it won't solve your problem.)

Tools

By placing metaphorical language outside of science, a whole set of possible solutions are excluded and, therefore, a whole set of problems as well.

It's like having a wooden beam that needs to be sawed, but the carpenter insists on using only the hammer. Since he will not be able to saw the wood with that tool, he says to himself: why saw the wood? I don't really need to saw the wood. This isn't my problem, he'll conclude.

For the foolish carpenter, his problems are the ones that he is able to solve with the tools he knows how to use. He doesn't start by looking around and detecting his problems. He starts by looking at the tools he knows how to use.

Tools and Apprenticeship

"With these tools, what problems can I solve?"
(This is a foolish question.)
"With these problems, what tools do I need?"
(This question is better.)
"With these problems, what tools do I need to learn how to use?"
(This question is better still: it presupposes intention and a plan of action.)

An Incompetence

Learn, therefore, to utilize metaphors, dear scientist. Don't be incompetent.

Disproportionate Methodologies

There is, in scientific methods—if we look deeply into them—a principle of proportion. Two on one side presupposes two on the other. If we see one side of the methodology, we can predict what the other side will be: it's equal to it. The disproportionate scientific method is considered to be a bearer of error.

"Straighten up your methodology," is always yelled whenever there is methodological criticism. This comes out of the principle that an erroneous methodology is a disproportionate methodology.

Proportionate Methodologies

It's clear that a scientific method can be crooked, can have one side larger than the other. And be effective.

Proportion and disproportion should not be criteria for validating a methodology or not.

But look closely, observe, reflect upon what you are seeing. A conclusion: science lives, almost exclusively (should I remove the "almost"?), on proportional methodologies.

Proportionate Truths

Of course, the exclusive utilization of proportionate methodologies can only result in proportionate conclusions and proportionate truths. To say:

"Your truth is disproportionate," is to say: your truth is not a truth.

Belief

Nevertheless, I believe that there are disproportionate truths.

Results and Instruments

From another point of view: we always utilize a ruler to measure straight lines and a protractor to measure angles.

Try switching them: the ruler to measure angles and the protractor to measure straight lines.

You will reach different results. Will they be false results?

I wouldn't say that. I would be more cautious. I would say that they are different results.

Conclusions and Methodologies

"That methodology is not adequate for that problem."
This sentence contains an error.
Which is that any methodology is always adequate for any given problem. Methodologies are, rather, adequate or not for determined objectives.

"If you want to come away with those conclusions, you shouldn't utilize that methodology."
(This sentence is more sensible.)

The Correct Result

If you want to obtain the following result: 10 centimeters of a table measured by a ruler are 10 centimeters on *that* ruler; then you should utilize the ruler.

If you utilize the protractor, you won't obtain this result; you'll obtain a different one.

Imagine, for example, that you obtain 25cm (you were moving the protractor in a certain way, trying to adapt it to your objective of measuring that space).

What is the correct result? 10cm or 25cm?

Answer: both results are correct. Measuring with a ruler, that piece of table measures 10cm, and measuring with a protractor in a certain manner, and with certain gestures, that piece of table measures 25cm.

Repetition of the Result

Obviously it is essential to determine the manner of proceeding with this measurement, just as it was determined that to measure a distance with a ruler, one shouldn't move the ruler, and that one must make the zero point of the ruler coincide with the zero point of the thing measured.

It is this that allows the methodology to be repeated precisely and, therefore, precisely to achieve the same result at two different moments.

Imagine, then, that you establish in detail the procedure to execute when you are measuring distance with a protractor.

With a determined and clear procedure, you could repeat the measurement as many times as you want—you will always obtain the same result.

And you have known, for some time, that it is the repetition of results that provides the scientist with the illusion of truth.

Therefore, if you repeatedly obtain a result of 25cm with your protractor, you will be convinced that you have the true result in front of you.

You could summarize science in the following way: I always obtain this result, therefore this result is true.

And you can already see that this thought is barely sensible. Be careful with it. (This thought can hypnotize.)

Possibility of Comparison

Think about this: what if you didn't have a ruler, if it had never been invented? If, to measure a piece of wood, you only had a protractor?

Can you say that the result obtained by the protractor measurement would be false? How could you prove that? What, then, would be true, lacking a point of comparison?

In fact, that measurement would be true.

Methodology and Truth

At bottom, we settle on a methodology that obtains a determined result, a determined value, and we call this fixed methodology Truth.
(And all else is Lie, is false, is error.)
But you could have settled on another methodology, and thus arrived at another result and, therefore, another truth.

Error and Truth (1)

Your truths and your scientific conclusions are directly linked to your methodologies.

In the absolute, nothing is true. Everything is true according to a certain methodology.

All hypotheses can be true, for we can find a methodology that makes them true.

"Give me a lie, and I will find a methodology capable of transforming it into truth."

The opposite is even easier:

"Give me a truth, and I will find a methodology capable of transforming it into a lie (or an error)."

Error and Truth (2)

There is only one methodology capable of turning a formula into a truth. And there are an infinitude of methodologies capable of turning a formula into an Error (or a lie).

Consensus of the Scientific Community

A truth (a law) does not express the consensus of the scientific community about a conclusion. Rather, it expresses the consensus of the scientific community about a methodology.
This is an important difference.

Methodology and Truth (1)

Truth exists in the methodology and not in the result, you could say. (It is a quality of one and not the other.)

Methodology and Truth (2)

You look at an object and say: it is blue, has the shape of a cube, and it is heavy. These are some of its qualities.

If you look at the result of a scientific thesis and say: *it is true*, you commit an error in the attribution of qualities. And if you look at a methodology and say: *it is true*, you commit yet another error in the attribution of qualities.

Methodology and Truth (3)

You should say, rather: the *belief* in truth is situated in the methodology and not in the result.

Or even: the belief in truth should be transferred from the result to the methodology.

(If you did this, you would be more conscientious than science.)

Machines and Thought

Machines are not merely an extension of the body, but an extension of thought.
You think more because you have machines; you think more through machines.

Tools

But the simplest Machine or tool—like a hammer, for example—is like a crystallized ratiocination. A thought has become fixed in a shape, and now that thought can be repeated innumerable times, without the necessity of stimulating the mind again.

A tool: fixed ratiocination with the capacity to be repeated until the material from which it is made is exhausted.

To Function and to Investigate

To function is to repeat a ratiocination. This is the hammer.
To investigate is to not repeat a ratiocination. This is difficult.

Instruments of Scientific Investigation

If the instruments utilized in scientific investigation are the fixing of an idea with an enormous capacity to self-repeat, then what can these instruments discover?

Or rather: can the repetitive detect the new?

If, on the other hand, the tools of a scientific investigation are a living ratiocination, which can still move, independent of the investigator, then who is doing the investigating: the investigator or the hammer utilized by him? Who thinks more?

"This machine is the best part of my brain" (this is a possible sentence).

Philosophers, Scientists, and Technology

The advantage of the philosopher in relation to the investigator surrounded by technology is that the former can say:
"I was the one doing the thinking."
Whereas you can accuse the latter, pointing to the machines:
"They were the ones doing the thinking."

God and Science (1)

There is no machine capable of detecting the Truth.

We can nevertheless think of a mechanism capable of proving that the results obtained by another mechanism are true or false. A machine that verifies methods and results. A machine that validates the criteria of the experiment. A machine that only produces two words or two digits: one that signifies: true; another that signifies: false.

After every investigation, the investigator would put the results and conclusions into that Truth Detection Machine, and it would respond: Yes or no, Truth or Lie. We would immediately toss the results in the trash or rejoice in the success (this would mark the end of that which is called "scientific discussions").

However, such a machine could only be built by God, and therefore it is first necessary to have a belief in God. Two beliefs, then: the belief in God, and the belief in the possibility of God having such a machine (and further still: a belief in the chiaroscuro nature of the World, a belief in the idea that everything is divided into true and false).

God and Science (2)

It is absolute impotence.
The only manner of definitive proof in science would be an effect of the existence of a machine made by God. A machine that divides in two (in True and False) the propositions of the World (language that men bring to the earth).
The truth that scientists seek can only be proven—absolutely, definitively—by a Machine made by God.

Brief Notes on Fear

Good/Evil

An attempt to introduce Good into Evil to correct the concentration of ingredients of what has already happened and what you do not want to be repeated. The danger, however, of this attempt is that the one and the other have, on the outside, the same color, identical physical qualities, and sometimes a physiognomy copied one from the other. And even because one dissolves in the other, like two substances that have lost the notion of laws and experience.

Darkness

In the dark, man sticks to his inclination to repeatedly not perceive things, in order to be free of anxiety: stupid and alone, like someone who believes in many things, but none of them tangible.

Confusion

We are in the world and we sniff out the essence of the city with an organ that is not the nose. Thus we confuse nauseating smells with others—those of the most beautiful spices and curiosities that are put on our plates or dabbed on our necks.

The Elect

No physiognomy belongs more to the community than that of the man elected by the express desire of his mortal companions. How this man will manage to smile afterwards, alone, is not the problem of his hurried fellow citizens. No immortality is complete, as is well known; and this incompleteness is warmly welcomed by grave-diggers and the weary; and even by the envious.

Nature

With water and soap one tries to rid stones of the persistent smell of nature, which, not succumbing, remains even after a long train trip, a ride up in a modern elevator, and arrival at a new apartment.

With this purchase, we threaten to begin a new life—you should remember this—but the fact is that the stench of the forest that the stone brings with it calms us down, demanding the abrupt and just diminution of expectations.

Modesty

One of the final attempts to demand, of ourselves, the persistence of a simple secret. However, modesty, like any other exotic gesture that a severe teacher first corrects and then eliminates, is not untouchable—sometimes it even turns into cement that the chisel of existence levels, redirects, and undoes.

The Absolute

What are we waiting for? The Absolute possesses one or two details that are covered by that which quotidian words would call blemishes; like bruises on a banged-up knee that refuse to go away—memory (with a perverse color) of a major occurrence. What, then, are we waiting for in order to cleanse ourselves—of these two, no more, blemishes that persist? We wait, simply because we are afraid of what will remain once we cleanse ourselves of them. Without at least the prospect of escape, the Absolute will never be tolerable for humans.

The Truth

We constantly modify the concentrations of Truth. A belligerent text is substituted in turn, in the following century, by a text that is, above all, peaceful, that, instead of fighting may even, who knows, tell stories—even if they are fictional. In fact, Truth isn't something that always accepts the same leash, the same owner, or that can even be called by the same name. Nor does it so much as run in the same manner—out of laziness, we could say, if we want to get ahead of ourselves—after the sticks that men amusedly toss into the distance. The fact is that sometimes (in certain centuries) this docile dog has a limp.

Intervals

We do not collect transitions—treks between one place and another. This incapability, for that is what we are dealing with, is, among others, one of the ones that devalues us the most. We tranquilly devalue—with internal nerves trained for just this task—one place and another, a feeling and what emerges afterwards, consecutive lovers, one day and the next (Sunday, Monday), but that which lies in between the visible, the nameable, and the memorizable is lost—without texture or even the minimal taking up of space that allows your collection to become credible in the eyes of others. And what we cannot display does not exist.

Myth

For centuries, Myth has left visible of itself only a little detritus, one or another well-told narrative. It comes out of History and a time when men had but weak instruments of measurement and attempted to enter the modern house through the front door, the one that everyone uses. The fact that they are now only allowed in through the servants' entrance is no reason, by itself, to accuse rational beings of having lost their capacity to be astonished. It's rather a reason to accuse Myth itself of a loss of virility, obvious from the way in which it sometimes seem to go from one place to another begging to be explained.

Problems, Answers

The raw material, so to speak, of an answer seems to be of lesser exchange value than that of the question. This if we place them—question and answer—in the marketplace of men for whom curiosity has taken a central place in their existence. However, as we well know, those men are a minority. All other marketplaces (and there are many) are predominately composed of men who make decisions about the life and death of others, men whose destiny has already shown them its unsurpassable tragic side; and in these other men, in these other marketplaces, an answer is the only value that can be transmitted. To their children, as an inheritance, these men will bequeath decisions and lifestyles; while as an offering to the people they hate, they will bequeath all that they were unable to answer in life—the way criminals leave the severed head of a horse on their enemy's doorstep in order to scare them.

The Immortals

Like a poet who strives to be praised for something else altogether—and not for that weakness that requires immediate courage—certain men insist on not waiting for death and, due to this distraction they are always caught—like an adulterous woman by her husband—in a state of disorder, bodies stripped bare, mistakenly revealing an immoral light that they always swore they didn't possess.

And because they are thus espied and—even worse—unable to make even the slightest gesture of modesty, those who feigned immortality make their final fall without a single preparation finished. They die at a moment of betrayal, whereas the old manuscripts advise us to end our lives in the position of one who is sacrificed, in the form of one whom others have deceived, whom others have defeated.

Melancholy

In the glass drunk while pondering the loss of a close friend, the dregs that remain therein are a mixture of an unpleasant mental sensation and the obvious presence of a liquid. This mixture causes a momentary hesitation that comes to an end with the return of your melancholic body to the world, or else, if all goes poorly, the attack—for the time being not entirely visible—of this same world upon your body, for time and circumstances have never tolerated someone who assumes that (just) because they are sad they have acquired the status of immortal.

The Correct Moral Philosophy

You await the correct moral philosophy the way a lover awaits his beloved in a train station. But the train is running late and you start to get nervous. You look at your watch over and over, then look at the empty tracks. And if you are impatient enough, you will soon give up, not on love, but on that particular woman. And you will then try, if possible, minutes later, to find another companion—who knows?—one of the others on the platform who cannot tolerate the wait for even a minute longer.

You will then certainly end up with a worse woman, one who will make your life come undone even more, and irreversibly so, but this is made up for in the long run—so you think—by how quickly you ceased to be alone.

Speaking, Listening

You treat the words you say as if they were first-class passengers and you were an obsequious employee, and, in the presence of the words of others, you behave as if they were the obsequious employee and you were the passenger traveling first class.

Morality (1)

Your morality, still quite green, only trains those muscles that will impede it from rotting. And such a training regimen, when it is successful, ensures your morality will die green as well, without a single answer—a morality that gesticulates in a neutral and indistinct state. Ultimately, just a girl who is too shy to abandon the corner of the room in which other, more daring girls dance and play, taking a risk that they might, at a fateful moment, stumble and look ridiculous or perverse. Like an overly shy girl, your morality will stay in the corner within you, waiting its turn.

Morality (2)

Thus, then—since nothing within you has rotted—you die content, as if you were born into a game and all of your actions were in the service of first discerning, politely, the rules, and only afterwards deciding which side you are fighting for and what the possible objectives and movements are. However, there are complex games whose rules appear to have been devised so that no mortal might ever discern them.

This is about playing the game, the world insistently tells you. But what are the rules?, you insistently ask the world. And the answer always ends up coming at the wrong moment, in the wrong place. Or else in a language of which you know two or three words, not even enough to choose a dish at mealtime.

Beauty

Among other effects, beauty, when it is countenanced, as long as it doesn't surpass certain bearable limits, diminishes the fear and disorientation that sometimes take hold of a man alone. You might not know precisely where you are on the map—be it geographical location or the more personal location in which you position yourself in relation to others—but at least you are in front of something beautiful—a woman, an animal, another man, a building. You don't have everything, of course—no one ever has—nevertheless you can at least assure yourself that you are not crazy, and here's the proof: the way someone separates the trash into different materials—empty bottles from food scraps, say—you separate that which is beautiful from that which is not. And to separate is, in part, to be lucid.

But nothing lasts long enough. At a certain point, that which is beautiful seems to have lost its color, and confronted with the collapse of something that had kept you company, you are left to confront yourself, like an enemy who has a gun at your back. This is not the best condition for not killing yourself.

Desistance

You do not understand the translation, into some far-off tongue, they made of your cry for help. You are faced with it as if faced with someone else's words. And, nevertheless, those words—in the original language, your language—were the most capable of placing you back into the world. Unable to recognize even the tone in which you screamed those words, and disgusted with the fact that they've translated your cry for help into an unknown language—you thus desist and, finally, politely accept the impossibility of someone hearing you.

Expectations

You perfect your expectations in such a way that when you arrive at old age you no longer expect anything from the world, from mankind, or from animals.

Illness

It is not about annihilating or domesticating; illness came, and you, like a good host, let it in, and even let it have the best chair in the house. But the fact is that the guest doesn't seem to want to get up, no indication has been revealed (and how many days have passed? Weeks? Months?) of anything akin to the beginning of a cordial and polite farewell. You look right at it, finally, from your increasingly uncomfortable chair, and look at it as if you were measuring, with your eyes, its strength and eventually its friends—thus vacillating between being rude, forcefully banishing it, and just accepting the circumstances with a certain attitude of good sportsmanship. And given your unusual courteousness, for which you've been praised since childhood, you grow partial to a different solution: you are the one, then, who gets up to leave, encouraging the illness to please eat the last of the food you have in the kitchen, and, after that, leaving, with a final look of understanding, the entire house at its disposal.

Losing your Mind

You want to decipher the way you used to think, but, as a means of doing this, you only have your own thoughts at your disposal. And they are older now, as if they had lost their physical dimension: height, width, length; and they've even lost their elasticity, their agility in leaping, their capacity to see what is on high when crawling, to see what has already found its proper place down below when jumping. With unsteady legs, thought attempts to understand why it started to run, where that initial, original impulse came from, and in which direction that movement was headed. If they get an answer, your thoughts forget about this evaluation of their own biography and, like prostitutes who have long ago lost their vigor and capacity of attraction, slouch down in their chairs. And instead of choosing the object of their action, they accept being chosen; and today, right now, like prostitutes in a dilapidated brothel, your thoughts are content (and how!) whenever some old man chooses them.

Children

You don't recognize the philosophy behind your children's actions and because of this you rail against the world, which has ruined that which you call family tradition—a shapeless thing composed of physical and mental habits, a few phrases that are repeated in the face of repeated situations, distinctive fears, audacious behaviors that you already know materialize whenever the intensity of the circumstances goes above a pre-determined limit, though still below yet another limit; and all this, which is a lot, has been ruined, you say, by that which you call the art—skillfully executed by others—of the tempest, art that beats, time and again, against the wooden post (which you planted firmly in the ground), weakening it to the verge of falling down.

However, your children say just the opposite about the past: there was no wooden post, there wasn't even any ground. They were lost and now, because they have no other, this is their spatial reference point: when they see you, when they sense your proximity, they retreat, head in a different direction.

You're alone, you claim, holding onto three broken wooden posts—which correspond to each of your children—and you remain seated next to that which was always your ground, and which you still intend to defend.

However, they aren't the only ones who look at you as if looking upon someone who, empty-handed, has fallen down, helpless. And just because—say your children, in stupid mockery—you don't look down doesn't mean you'll stop falling.

Growing Old

Like that which, from afar, looks like a dog with a domesticated head on its shoulders and, from up close, suddenly acquires the dangerous mysteriousness that monsters carry with them—the shapelessness that frightens and disgusts because you don't know which end bites and which end of the fur defecates—, intractable, beauty escapes immediately after it is captured.

The way, however, in which it resists capture is beauty's manner, not of fleeing, but of letting itself be. That which escapes is not, then, the beauty of the thing observed—mind you—but rather the observer himself, who, like an animal threatened by something stronger, flees. With more arrogance than scientific difficulties, confusing physiological weakness with the world's weakness, this is the man who believes that beauty fades. But no: it is passed on from you, who are growing old, to him, who is starting to be young.

Against Rashness

You are alive, and there is a fundamental flaw—not having died yet cannot be, can never be, ultimately, the end-all, be-all of satisfactions.

The Only Reason to Be in a Hurry

A thing that can never be made permanent in a drawing: this is the element that you have pursued ever since you became lucid; ever since you understood that no object, man, or animal, is some immortal thing that merely allows itself to be seen out of kindness. And, because you can't draw it, you're in a hurry.

True Occupation

To continue to give shape to that which remains hidden in darkness (and which you have never seen) could be considered inconsequential stubbornness, but, also, the purest of the sculptor's actions.

Calm Down!

Even if you descend to a place in which you can no longer see the clarity of the surface, don't worry too much, because the surface of the world—it too—will be dark in just a few hours (night is drawing near).

Apprenticeship

At the edge of a precipice, upside down, held at the ankles by your most illustrious teacher, thus the apprentice, frightened, repeats the morning's lesson.

The Conflagration

In the middle of the fire that is destroying the cathedral, a man still attempts, for the last time, to contemplate, amid the smoke, the harmony of forms that for centuries that building imposed and transmitted to him. In the midst of all the screaming and commotion of movement, someone demands from him a different action and, peppered with insults, unenthusiastically taking hold of the bucket of water handed to him, it is then that, finally, like someone who is thrown, helpless, from their own horse, the man participates in the collective, but useless, attempt at salvation.

Differences

If while you allow yourself to be caressed by idleness you can, from afar, be mistaken for a dog, when you arise into action, the differences will become obvious, running the risk of allowing yourself to be considered human.

The Threat

The endeavor to bury a house up to its very top, like a body, is more violent than the mere destruction carried out by explosive engineering. (Beneath fabric or soil), much more threatening than ruins is that which, maintaining its energy intact, tries to hide itself. (When you destroy, you diminish the power of that which was previously unified; when you cover up, you increase this power.)

Lucidity

At the banquet to which you were unexpectedly summoned you search for the right words and discourse, and, for this reason—since by attempting to present yourself as human, you forgot about the food, insulting the appetite— you will never be invited again.

Can an artist speak this way about his or her own life? Certainly. However, no one who is lucid would want to go back and live some other existence—no victual is that tempting.

Secret

Far from the vulgar gaze, hidden beneath the earth like the root of some plant, don't forget to retain something; that only after your death does the world perceive your dimensions.

To Read, Repeating Movements

Between the right hand and the other hand of the same man, there is sometimes an obscure distance. This is not about one body part hiding intentions or even actions. It's something else.

When, to welcome someone, you open your arms, the aforementioned distance increases and the hand, on either end, signals a certain manner in which your body is spreading. When the embrace materializes and, at the other person's back, your hands finally reunite, they formalize a symbol that is at once bleak and hopeful: for only behind the back of the other do your two body parts unite with an energy that is worthy of admiration. Give it a try: without another body in the middle, bring your hands together forcefully, or even violently, and you'll see how ridiculous it is, you'll notice the difference in intensity.

Yet sometimes—as you well know—there is no other body.

Thirty-Five Years (1)

One doesn't intend to eat like a character in a script does, having already, before the play begins, eaten his or her fill—however, sometimes existence renders one weary.

False Victory

Trained to caress, meticulously, every word of a book with his or her thought, the critical philosopher—through the system that introduces explications—seeks, in a manner that is not delicate, though it be legal, to reduce the arrogance that is inherent to the nature of any work of art. When this is achieved, it is because the work of art has failed.

Nevertheless, at the same time, it is at the very moment of this victory that the analyst, from top to bottom, has a better understanding that he or she has also failed. Every one of his or her victories is an additional defeat—and if there is no limit to one's tolerance for advancement, there is a limit, as is well known, to one's tolerance for defeat.

Thirty-Five Years (2)

As in an unexpected forest, after childhood you are in the world on the hunt for differing varieties of happiness. If you are exceptionally effective and have a refined aim, you will soon catch all the possible varieties that exist in the forest. And afterwards nothing shall remain except an unbearable sensation that, even if you cease to be lost, what you will find, or what will find you, will be even worse.

At a certain point, the alternative is to remain lost in the forest, to wander aimlessly, or to be found, eventually, by the rabid pack of wolves that had long before picked up the scent of a wound.

How to Live?

Guided, simultaneously, by a slow animal and a fast one, the wagon, unbalanced, will end up falling to one or the other side—and the manservant, who had been holding the whip, will blame the accident on the slower animal, while the noble lady in the carriage behind, will not hesitate to blame the fast one.

The Thief

As the painter looks out on the world, she decides which colors, upon retreating from this world, she will put on the canvas. We are dealing with a theft (an educated one) of light and its different angles of incidence, but it is evident that only in an artificial cave may an artist practice her craft.

Removed, you no longer see what you were seeing when you were removing yourself, just as close up you no longer see what you were seeing when you were coming closer. You do what you do at a remove from the world; and you receive indispensable material to remain able to remove yourself from it and come closer to it, over and over, like a thief who only steals that which she cannot take hold of—the essential, therefore.

Observer's Error

After the third marvel, the observer grew tired and, demanding above all else events that were different from previous ones, and full of curiosity, he headed towards a spot from which he could see the stuff that mediocrity produced. Meanwhile, on the other side, the marvels continued until the moment when, sad that no one was there to watch them, they stopped, desisting at once.

Education by Blood

Circulating across the surface of the earth, the final philosophical system stops in the face of a horrendous crime, and there are stripped from it the certainty, the ultimate formula, the positions, and the rigorous distances that this system established as fashionable for the good and intelligent heart of man to possess in relation to events.

As if crimes, and the mere witnessing of them, were ultimately powerful means of understanding, resolute revelations, vestiges of the ancient and instantaneous lessons that classical wise men dispensed, individually, to each of their scarce and rigorously selected students.

Beneath the Earth

We are in the realm of minutiae, and it is here that the worm apportions its appetite. Over time: patiently or, if you will, slowly. And over space: with the minute rigor of leaving no part unexplored.

Like the gods, in certain origin myths, worms know by eating; devouring as apprenticeship.

Preparation for Battle

In the middle of an interminable warehouse you request a weapon or any tool with which to confront whatever is coming this way; however, all that they give you is a map, not of the outside world, but of the exact space you find yourself in.

If you're lucky, you'll never again find the door that leads to the world and thus, combat-free and forgotten, you'll defeat, unwounded, the most powerful of enemies.

The hooves of raging horses can hardly be heard, and there are those who say they never existed at all, and yet you long ago decided to make preparations.

Expectations

Intrigued by a certain potency that one can feel coming from the other side of a door that years ago someone locked up forever, hiding or destroying the key, placing against the door's structure heavy and insurmountable materials, thus it is that the great singer ceases to sing, the great athlete to run, the great orator to speak, the great fighter to fight—and even the great philosopher rests his hands atop the desk, demonstrating that he has formally ceased to think.

On the other side of this door that no living being has ever seen open is a thing—a living thing—with an inaccessible form, function, and language, which, nevertheless, also, for a long time, for many, many years, has given up.

Enviable Life

Indecipherable is the man who, in addition to remaining silent and motionless, hides himself from the light, like the oldest rat.

Of this man—for having never been seen, but, above all, for having never been understood—a robust and luminous statue will be built in the center of the city, which cannot even recall if anyone ever witnessed his birth.

Systems of Comprehending the World

In systems of comprehending the world, there can also sometimes be seen contractions and relaxations like the visible common muscle of a mammal. As is well known, contraction almost always tends toward action; and when, on the other hand, the muscle relaxes, it is because it is afraid of nothing, the ambience that surrounds it does not disturb it, and as such, taken to the limit, it may even fall asleep. As a cursory study of corporal physiology demonstrates, successive relaxations, without intervals of tension or contraction, cause a slow, but unequivocal, decay of tissues.

Without the visible presence of adversaries, muscles meticulously prepare their own defeat.

Against Specialization

Located beside a bedridden patient, a wide window that completely occupies the space of an entire wall becomes perverse.

But how can you explain this to someone who doesn't confuse architecture with metaphysics?

Phrases That Are Spoken from a Distance

Such a phrase never coincides with an unhappy moment: suffering is an object to be known, some claim; always those who haven't suffered for a long time or those who have yet to suffer. Danger.

Nothing is as dangerous as to have accomplished all your tasks for the day and it still be morning, to have accomplished all of your tasks in life and still not be dead.

Calling Attention

Nothing is in the background. It is your position that bestows a hierarchy on the position of things.
But this consideration may also be placed behind many other considerations.

Cry for Help

That which you call a cry is merely a short phrase verbalized in a convincing tone. If you hear it as a cry, you will lead it to an eventual salvation; if you hear it as it is, a synthesized formula of knowledge, you will, like an attentive novice, sit at the foot of the man who spoke, trying to decipher the most important component. You will wait, then, carefully and patiently, for the next cry.

A Reason to Do It

If you don't make haste to the locale, you will never know if the person who is crying for help wants to receive it or give it.

Miracle and Repetition

In those ceremonies and rituals which repeat—with short intermissions and extreme detail—an assemblage of movements and verbal formulae, you feel as if you are in a farce—someone promises you, weekly, that which no human in this life can give.

To Live

Attacked along his path by bandits that rob and abuse him, a man, surviving, returns at last to his home to prepare the next trip.

On the Lowest Hypothesis for Remaining Human

Between animal and man, you clearly distinguish, looking only at the outside, the head of one from the other; the tail, which never appears on the human; the clothes, which never have the adequate dimensions for the animalian—even if the measurements are rigorously correct; and even the manner of speaking, of course, which in one—in man—can be expressed in thousands of languages and sounds, and in the other—in animal—is similar to infantile verbal scribbles. You know, therefore—even when observing distractedly—to say—and how this makes you proud!—: there goes the man and there, down below, the animal.

Nevertheless, sometimes it is the gestures—of one and the other—that you mix up. In such a way that, if it were possible to conceive of two types of beings with neither form nor language, but still with movement, man and animal would belong—you swear—to the same tendency; the tendency, almost a desperate one, to love some things and flee from others. If we set aside, you say, aesthetics and sentences, we will be in the presence of a community of desires and fear.

And this demonstrates that—if you will—in no time you'll be able to slither like the most agile of reptiles.

Chance

As if from the mouth of a madman, who has been devoid of reason for years, there suddenly issued forth a verbal formulation finally capable of explaining the world, certain chance meetings bring together, definitively, and after many years of despair and divergence, a man and woman.

Being Alive

With both feet not only resting on Mystery, but inside it as if submerged—in such a way that you are already doubting if, underneath that opaque and incomprehensible pellicle, they still exist and belong to you—you advance your torso, attempting to keep at least your hand out of the reach of this force about which you know neither origin nor limits.

Like someone saying goodbye when taking leave of a person she loves and doesn't know if she'll see again, you move your right hand, which appears, like the sleeve of an ordinary shirt, on the outside of the Mystery into which you fell without being invited or desiring to be so. But in fact your hand does not bid farewell to anyone—perhaps it is calling for help.

Notebooks of Gonçalo M. Tavares | 22

Brief Notes on Connections
(Llansol, Molder and Zambrano)

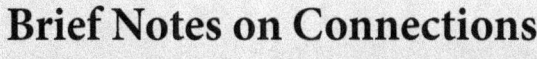

This book is obviously dedicated to María Zambrano, Maria Filomena Molder, and Maria Gabriela Llansol, three writers whose work demands from us a response, a parallel movement, a dislocation." . . . the commentary of the parallelist is as limitless as the text is limitless; and the text, whether it be traversed in its structure by echoing spaces, or treated as a labyrinth of all possible itineraries, is absolutely limitless."

GIORGIO MANGANELLI

"Is nonexistence always stronger?" (MGL)

Deep down, that which exists has already proven its weak intensity. After childhood, the universe is only interesting to the absent-minded. So then: to welcome the invisible as the only remarkable news.

A woman grabs her pillow and decides to travel. Travel as the concept of stopping very quickly. To stop at great speeds is to travel attentively.

Falling asleep as a way of knowing. As if dreams were science for the precise gaze of someone asleep.
Theory doesn't always come from will. Sometimes it comes from the turning off of will. Intention forgotten, man knows. Like someone falling.
Knowing as a manner of falling. Knowing as if confronted with a surprise. Not investigating: to have the surprise of knowing.

Eyes become frightful when there is nothing to see. Like a weapon kept in a drawer, perilously.

The danger of organs resigned, through circumstance, to uselessness. They await and affirm hatred. Eyes, out of boredom, when there is nothing to see (when the visible is mere repetition), become diabolical.

"Active forgetting is one of the conditions of movement" (MGL)

Forgetting is something that happens. Like an artisan who dictates the shape of a chair to the neutral wood that awaits it.

Movement is an animalistic and intellectual action. A muscular state of ratiocination. As if, in fact, ratiocination had cells; which it has.

All ratiocination as the concrete disposition of electrons. Minute particles find themselves at the foundation of a philosopher's theory, particles visible only through instruments that brutally enlarge reality.

Because the theory does not exist or, if it exists, is thick and has volume: nothing is so large that it doesn't contain within it smaller, minute things. A large thing that only has this dimension—a large hollowness—is difficult to imagine. A large hollowness would collapse on top of itself, disappear, become minuscule.

The necessary conditions for the life of a particle can be summed up thusly: absence of death. All the conditions and qualities of life disappear in a split second with this lone appearance. Death, without qualities, annuls all the qualities of existence.

"He will absorb the love of tragedy, liberating him from the event" (MZ)

Culture defined as a distancing from the event. I know because I have distanced myself.

How to understand that which makes contact, at this moment, with our body?

To be touched is to ignore.

Heightened ignorance: love and pleasure. Lowered ignorance: to be attacked; a punch, a shove.

To know is the result of an exact distance in relation to the event. If one is *very close* to the event, one does not know it, suffers from its influence; if one is *very far*, one also does not know it, and because one nearly cannot see, one nearly forgets.

A measurement between one who knows and that which is known. If the thing to be known takes off running, the person who knows should also run. A motionless man has no theories.

The essential event is not corrupt, that is: it cannot be bought. However, manifold minor events can be bought. Money makes things happen (the simplicity of the proposal: *I pay you to do this.*)

We can say: money makes more things happen (in greater quantity) than luck or chance.

"There is a list of days, like the table of contents of a book" (MGL)

Thus old people and their nostalgic syllabi: a list of days with habitual connections and predetermined feelings.

Life as an individual work that escapes the control of the artist. Luck/chance as an outside artist who comes to chisel her ephemeral will into our path.

An individual work that breathes and is not alone. That is being alive.

MFM	"Quite powerful are the forces of the night, which work in the multiple blackness, in the intense immobility of the night."	In nature, work is not paid, simplistic observation of man.	Night is manifested in a drawer.	Respect your fear. Keep it closed.
MGL	Transform myself "into a species of I-less poem"	The most obvious I is in the looks that others shoot towards us. These are the things that give us an identity. It's false, this identity, but at least it is one.	Take note: a photograph is false evidence. That, which you say is me, that, at least, I am absolute certain is not me.	Your body appears when you get dressed. When you flee, without having any that you're doing so, your immobility is great. The body is not that obvious.

Brief Notes on Connections | 223

| MZ | "Inspiration is necessary even in thought." | Thought is an event. Like a disaster or the strange appearance of someone who doesn't want to let you return to the place from which you came. | Thought is a humiliated passion; it is passion after it has been humiliated. | The strongest thoughts are those that find themselves close to the structure of a declaration of love. You look for the words and their sequence, but the point of origin is a feeling. I am feeling so much that I might even be able to think, says someone. |

"... movement of putting the fact into the pains of difficulty, not accepting its obviousness" (MFM)

Two pieces of evidence show themselves to be mutually false when displayed. Because the only evidence would be an entire thing, without any remainder, without any other. Evidence identifies itself with the complete universe, and thus places a full stop on difficulties. On the contrary, to be alive is to be *in a difficult place*.

But the ancient historical facts haven't come to an end: every new event adds, centuries later, new difficulties to what has occurred. A creator is one who puts problems in the past. Like someone who, with their feet, shows respect to the great dates of a country, while, with their hands, decides to invent a new form.

Because every invention is a heresy, it jeopardizes the present and even events that have already entered into the world of documentation. To invent is to destroy documents. Similarity of apparently opposite actions: to lift up and to drop.

The problem with History is that it wasn't written by an artist. It was written, as much as possible, in a democratic, consensual manner, *by a majority*. Perhaps one of specialists, but a majority nonetheless. The History of a country is written after the voting is done.

Those who are certain that the events took this shape, vote X.

Those who are certain that the events took on this other shape, vote Y.

Not even dates are exact.

The great difficulty doesn't result from errors, but from precision. Exactitude jeopardizes. Being precise destroys.

Because the artist does not open boxes. The artist classifies them as material from the past. But somewhere, in a closed box, is a grand invention that hasn't yet been discovered.
The artist opens, then, the box of invention.

Not all closed boxes are historical.

A certain contemporary manner of seizing upon the historical book.
Take note: in Winter, the human has only hands, face, and nape out in the open air. In Winter, man is less natural, you'll say (*he is touched less* by nature).

Nature is a thing that touches, but in the city everyone is convinced that nature is merely something that can be touched.
If it were a game, you would ask: who touches the other more often, who touches with greater force than the other—man or nature?
But how to be inside and push against the inside? No human is so fast that they cease to be nature.

A tall object is not always an obstacle. Sometimes it is the smallness of the thing that disrupts our advance.

In war, translations are more violent, *more sentimental.* The man who arrives at what was once his home sees the tattered remains of a jacket and cries. Small material vestiges are translated into emotions.

Those consumed with language will say: all translation between tongues should be rational, exact, never emotional.

This man, on the contrary, will say: *I cannot be exact when I am hurting.*

We only start to be alive when it stops being easy.

"I did the exercise of the fear of death" (MGL)

Thinking about the owners of things. Who said it?
Not having goods, only bads.

Resting upon the void are hands without fear.
For my own good, I don't have any goods. Thus the cruelty of the Stoics confused with the perversity of names.

"We shall die exhausted and strong" (MGL)

Exhausted like someone who has not yet loved or exhausted like someone who now begins to hate.
And the strength comes from the weakness of others. You are strong in comparison, the same way you are tall or short.

Nudity identical to *being dressed in space*. Ascetics make no noise when they enter the water, a subtlety of philosophy: they don't enter, they become common, water is the chosen substance.
The "quantity of soul" (MFM) is not divisible like other quantities; it proceeds as a whole and disappears without leaving a trace.

Complaints
"Complaining about the recollection the nostalgic longing: having already seen, having already seen." (MFM)
What can a man who has already seen do, if not accept blindness?
A good chunk of the world is already in my stomach, what follows will be a loss. How to live without the instinct of conquest?
Two men pass by on either side of a madman. And he is cured.
"While my gaze learned how to make poems." (MGL)   The gaze is not a final occurrence. It is an action that directs, that plans, that accepts the present moment and the following day.   How many times do you look at what you love?   After love is secured, you will cease to look.   Terrible news for love as well: "having already seen, having already seen."   And the man who rejoices runs through the streets: still haven't, still haven't seen!
"Perhaps philosophy will not destroy piety?" (MZ)

Energy

The energy of a bicycle is exterior to it. An object that, when still, threatens movement, but threatens in a manner opposite of the threat of a seated man's legs. The energy of the legs is not exterior. It isn't beside them. It is not a laterality of the thing.

"I know very little about what it is to have" (MGL)

Copulation: two distinct things simulate a connection that, at every moment, threatens to rupture, until the moment at which it definitively ruptures.

Sacrifice: to fall asleep when someone has just opened the door: sacrificing curiosity.

"The thoughts we keep to ourselves are lost" (MFM)

Lilith carries a razor in her hand to sharpen an idea. A mythological razor, possessor of an immaterial, yet intense cut; an invisible exactitude doesn't cease to be exact.
It is not an *insane efficacy*.

But efficaciousness is not an object that you can grasp and store away. If it were, all living beings would be efficacious. Efficaciousness is housed in time, not in space. And what does not exist in space cannot be stored away. That which inhabits time is untouchable and is the most essential. That which you can store away is not important; that which has volume, height, and length can be stored away.

Thoughts inhabit time. They use time in order to exist, just as fruit uses the tree in order to exist. There is no ground upon which thoughts rest, unless you consider the brain to be a compact institution, from which things never fall.

Writing, drawing: they are obvious occupations of space. Of that lean space that is a page, but still space.
An idea that is neither drawn nor written does not occupy space, it occupies time. The brain is a space in which many temporal phenomena occur.

An idea does not have a right or left side. It has neither weight nor volume, shape nor color. An idea has seconds, or minutes, sometimes hours, or entire days, months.

An idea is not curved, not straight.

Lilith traversed an open coffin, ran from one side to the other of the open coffin. Just two meters long: two strange sensations: running in such a small space and such intense movement inside a coffin that was made to store immobility. A philosophical exercise: *running inside a coffin*.

At night, Lilith was a woman who made noise with her ideas. She disturbed the neighbors.
Turn down the volume of those ideas, someone said.
A loud idea, a soft idea.
The interesting thing about intelligence is the way in which it seizes on any object. Things not only have a handle, like a teacup, the things in this world are also capable of being handled at every side, at all times, and by the strangest of instruments: from a hand, to tweezers, to the many kinds of forceps or pliers. We are being grasped at every side, as if we were crazy or as if we let others be crazy on us.
Do you want to be crazy on me?
Thus the most generous permission: Lilith allowed everyone to place their individual insanity on her.
You are free to be crazy, I won't tell anyone.
Only great friendships allow insanity.
Insanity *as a test*.
I don't yet know if you're my friend because I haven't been crazy yet.

Dialogue (1)

Maria Filomena Molder	Maria Gabriela Llansol
"Seal of property"	"The all dispersed, never again to be all"
"The light of the world marches through what exists"	"or a table on which to place god"
"Let's restart in another manner"	"... uses thought against that which is felt."
"Thinking means walking precisely toward one who is waiting for us."	"Intimately refined in solitude"
"... diction of the world ..."	"Day without intelligence"
"A battle for clarity"	"One is not transformed through clarity, one is transformed through inquietude"

"For life is this inability of an organ to disconnect itself from another" (MZ)

Inability to disconnect. I am alive: impossible to separate myself.
Or: I am alive: I am obligated to connect myself.

For Lilith, *the connections* between things were material cells that existed between things. If someone sits in a chair, it is because there are material, objective cells between the body of the person sitting and the chair.
Not in the chair or the body, but between these two things: there are cells.
We are not dealing with air here—air is neutral—but rather with a force that exists in the air.

Give, therefore, due importance to these cells. Take note: it's something like this: they do not belong to a concrete thing, A or B, they don't belong to anything; cells not of one thing, but of a function. They belong to an activity and not to a surface. They make connections possible.
Things draw near each other. And even: things *retreat from each other.*

Because retreating is still a movement of connection, a movement that proves the existence of connections with the other; if I retreat it is because there is something from which I'm retreating.

I am alive because I connect and I am alive because I retreat.

Death is neutrality, the impossibility of drawing near or retreating. The impossibility, as well, of maintaining the same distance. There is no distance, therefore there isn't even a maintaining of distance.

Being dead is not being able to flee from or hold on to something, but it is also not being able to stay in the same place.

You are not in any place, *you are dead.*

What, then, is lacking in our intelligence in biology? Technical instruments capable of seeing the signs of connection between things.

The proof that we are alive—the chair just as much as the man who sits in it—is not found in the living cells of each of these things, but rather in the cells that impede these two things from disconnecting. Because a man, even when he is out in the street, does not disconnect from the chair that is in his bedroom.

"There are secrets that demand to be published, and those are the ones that visit the writer making good use of her solitude" (MZ)

When a secret is published, you say: this is poetry.

A secret *is a thing that you did not know.*
Line of poetry: a secret that has just been made explicit.

It isn't a fact that you didn't know, it isn't a moment. It is a concrete thing, a thing that exists, like a stone.
A thing that you didn't know existed now finally exists in the world, it's here. This is the map of its localization, this is the line of poetry.
A secret *is a stone that you did not know.*

Lilith took hold of a secret the way she took hold of a man: she let herself latch on and stopped exerting herself.
Pull with force until you are embraced, she said.
To be embraced is to stop exerting yourself.

Secrets are only revealed on top of a mountain. It's not enough to publish a secret, you have to make it *general.*

General, generalized like certain heavenly bodies: the Sun, the Moon.

For example: the sky is a generalized secret. What do you know of the sky?

I see it so much that I don't know how to describe what I see.

Describe the sky? I'm incapable of doing it because *it never leaves my sight*.

It's as if you asked me to describe my own body.

Adorno, in his *Aesthetic Theory*, speaks of the "shudder of the New."

The New is an interruption.

You could say: after a prolonged silence, every word is new. Or say: after a long and vast emptiness, everything is new. Even if it is a stone *anew*, again.

You will define old age as that which is capable of saying, with disdain, the phrase: the New anew!

Living beings who have grown tired of the New. Please, don't bring me anything tomorrow.

"The art of putting bodies in danger" (MGL)

A hero like one whose stable situation is Danger.
I am safe: threaten me.
To be safe with yourself, to be in harmony: surround yourself with enemies.
Only in the face of the enemy do I establish amity with life itself.

You are a friend of your own life, you've made friends with your path.
To be *a friend of my own decisions*, that's the difficulty.
To make friends with the succession of my yeses and nos.
(the multiform variants)
I am the enemy of my yeses and my nos.
I am the enemy of my yeses and friend of my nos.
Friend of my yeses, enemy of my nos.
(the multiform variants)
This expression: *multiform variants*. It's a little like saying: the many many.
The opposite could be: the selfsame variant or: the *one multiform*.
This thing that is always the same varies a lot.
Monotonous surprise.

"The art of putting bodies in danger" (MGL)

The art of multiplying a unity, yet keeping it as one.

How many variations of One?
How many different ways to not-die?
A person can die in infinite ways: heart disease, shooting, stabbing, fall from a mountain, etc.
But can you not-die in different ways?
You will say: there's only one way to not die, it's to stay alive.
Very well, someone said.
But no, it isn't quite like that.

"The body, long and naked, has always been the continuation of a venom, or vice-versa" (MGL)

"To cure language" (Vicente Franz Cecim)
1—"pensive city"
2—"Born of the distrust of the mountains"
3—"33, the age at which one goes up on the Cross. I didn't want to go up on the Cross, I wanted to go beneath the fig tree."
4—"There is only the Ancient. The New is human vanity."

Lilith grabbed the venom and shook it. The way you do with a sheet covered in crumbs.
You die more through the mouth than through touch. In the case of venom.
But death is a function of touch, it's an effect that touches. It isn't tasted or smelled or seen. Death isn't something that comes in through the eyes like the color or shape of a thing. Death touches. You die because you have a sense of touch. You could lack all the other senses, but with the sense of touch, we are mortal.

You are immortal only if you cannot be touched.
You are mortal only if you can be touched.

But take note: the past cannot be touched. Try touching something that happened yesterday or six centuries ago. The past is untouchable, immortal.
Since it already ended, it never ends. How strange, you'll say.
But death comes in different material states. Death can come about in a gaseous state; in liquid state (poisoned water); or solid state: a mortal solid (knife, bullet).
As if death had *different temperatures*.
As if death were a substance that tolerated large variations in temperature. In extreme cold and extreme heat: it proceeds.

But, on a cold day, one requests that death come at a high temperature. *To compensate*, someone will say.

"Moved by the expectation of finding" (MFM)

Expectation is an elegant way of affirming that something is not happy in the time in which it finds itself	Only the unhappy hope.	Bachelard ("Earth and Reveries of Will") writes: "Perhaps we could educate ourselves to combat our weight, to cure ourselves of our weight."		The weight does not jump when we jump, the weight disappears when we jump.
To find is to be joyful, to be joyful is to have found.				To be sad is the same as having lost something.

		But, lost in the forest, a man sometimes jumps for joy.	The man who has become lost from other men sometimes finds things.		Things are found by men who have become lost.
"The praise of the particular, of the detail and its power" (MFM)					The detail does not leave space for you to look at other things.
		To find is to lose that which, moments before, you had.	You only find if you feel something missing.		To find a hole—the absence of things and even of space, of ground—to find a hole could be important.

I found a place where there are no things.				I found something that revealed an absence. Absence is presence in another space.	
Lilith had disastrous tendencies and a chair made of pinewood.		Lilith appreciated animals and numbers.			Lilith entered into a symbol and enlarged it until it became visible and material. After, she said: now it no longer interests me.
"A victory often makes one lonely," the Emperor says, and Joseph Brodsky writes.		Now understand the groups: those who lost draw near each other.			"Your intelligence will be what your habitual ideas have made of it," (Marcus Aurelius)

Dialogue (2)

María Zambrano	Maria Gabriela Llansol
"Walk in search of your crime"	"That what I desire to be teaches me"
"Living here, looking from here, defining."	"This house will only be a House if I write books here; for now, it is disarray and dust—"
"How is error possible? How can truth ably reside?"	"'Why doesn't he come to me?', I wanted to know. 'Because he is the one who has you in his surprising corner.'"
". . . poetry . . . without error or truth"	". . . I wanted to go inside the wood in order to know."
"In boundless space, man wants to orient himself with sacred actions. The first thing that occurs to him isn't to think, but to do. There is something in doing that is more passive than in thinking."	
"To define is the highest intellectual form of decision. To define is to make history."	"What was different found itself in front of the different and greeted it, exclaiming: 'Oh!'"

Whether fiction is a movement or an immobility

"To be waiting to become a plant, to recall having been an animal, to have come from far away to wait: to become, that is: to obtain your rest."

(Maria Filomena Molder)

hypothesis 1—*A fiction is a movement*

In certain kingdoms, patience is the principal form of muscles. The Plant Kingdom.

Let's say that the truth might be thought of thusly: something that exists and in the place where it exists, waits. And we, the ones who move (or rather: mortals), search for the place where what is immortal does its waiting.

Plato, you'll say.

Fiction, fictions, or rather: the hypotheses of truth would thus be movements. Movements that try to achieve immobility. That is: that place where one waits.

The truth, then: a Kingdom where there only exists the One; like the Vegetable Kingdom, in a certain way, where patience is the fundamental principle, but in which (contrary to what happens with weeds and roses) there is neither death nor growth. The truth does not distribute different intensities over time, nor does it recognize hierarchies of weakness. It neither asks for help nor gives aid. But if the truth is a place and that place is motionless, and if each fiction is a movement, then all the fictions are equal in their quantity of truth, for truth has no more than two quantities: Yes or zero. Because it is a paradox to think of a partial immobility. It is disturbing to say *swift immobility*.

hypothesis 2—*A fiction is an immobility*

But the truth can also be *an isolated object in motion*. And we can still associate the word "patience" with this movement. Patient movement. Movement that waits.
Truth as a movement that waits to cross paths with fiction. Only this. And fictions as immobilities: as motionless things. But because they are not complete (that is: true), they are impatient. Fiction as a thing that is impatient and motionless.
And the restless immobility of each fiction is seen, from above, as a dot. And fictions, taken together, as impatient immobilities that can be multiplied infinitely, never crossing paths, however, with the calm and constant movement that is truth.
A bit of Heraclitus, you'll say.
(Of course the only way to perceive nature is to simplify what Men have said about it. At a certain moment

in History, knowing ceased to be the effect of writing, painting, and drawing, and became an effect of erasing. A definition of poetry? Perhaps. Remove all the words from a sentence that nature does not require, this is a possible definition for poetry. For its function, for its endeavor.)

But

But what if truth were, ultimately, something that comes from afar and must be awaited? Movement that only thinks about staying still, about making the modification of position and of minutes unnecessary (space and time as two names for the same subject: impatience).
And if truth were a movement that will only find its waiting place at the moment when there doesn't exist a single path that doesn't coincide with the multiple fictions that already exist. Or rather: and if truth were only motionless (only extant) at the moment when fictions occupy the entirety of the map except for this *point*.
And if?
Every poet, like every sensible person, can only believe in this, which is two things: either truth is revealed to us or, if it is constructed, it remains for us to multiply fictions infinitely so that truth is seen surrounded on every side and *surrounded by all times*, immobile, hunted down like an animal.
A long process. Eternal? But a process; that is: we can do it.
Revelation doesn't depend on you; the construction does depend on you. And every sensible person only does what depends on them.
And, of course, truth being completely surrounded by

infinite fictions, what remains is a passageway that is far from easy, violent even, the essential passageway from surrounding something to being inside something, or to being something. Who will say that the end of History is not this: we construct, step by step, all fictions, all of the possible hypotheses, we make infinite marks on the map until the map becomes one single mark, with the exception of the white point that patiently awaits because it can no longer move: truth[1]. And there, surrounding the end (another name for truth) the way we stand around a well, leaning over the wall that delimits the end the way we lean over the wall that delimits a well, there we remain, motionless, lacking the strength to move, with only the weakness of contemplation. Waiting, in sum, patiently, for that which also waits for us in the same manner, patiently.

And thus History will end: man and truth waiting for the other to take the last step. They came from far away to obtain their rest, the final one. As in a duel.

(A final consideration. If you stay there for a long time, about take the last step towards truth, patiently, waiting, or rather: about to. If you remain like that for a long time, when you finally act, that last step will not be the last, but rather the first, for so much time has passed that all the other steps have been forgotten. And it all starts over again.

You will say, then: memory is necessary. I will say: courage is necessary.)

"What creates the highest sensuality is the distribution of light" (MGL)

Disrupting the amount of sun that reaches objects and its angle of inclination, clouds end up interfering with the sensuality of women and the sensuality of all creative animals.

Lilith is made up of a sensible substance, that which we commonly call human. Human substance is skeptical in relation to the landscape, looks at it from the outside, as if it were from another era, as if between the neutral landscape and the virile man who interprets there existed a difference of centuries. The landscape that surrounds me is not from my century, is not from my time.

Lilith knows that if you touch, for extended periods of time, the shadow of an object, your hand will be marked by that error; as if a hand, as it raises out of the shadow, brought with it an obsession, a dangerous mixture of what belongs to the human and what belongs to the night.

The distribution of light in a city depends on the philosophical and individual work that each citizen develops (this is a hypothesis). Brutes and naïfs will have the right to a reduced urban light.

If, on a street, at street number 25, second floor on the right, there lives a philosopher, the city and its electric light maintenance services should take care to direct great quantities of individual electricity to that place.

However, ninety percent of the city will remain in the dark.

"To put it another way: is it possible that thought wants to go back to being taught by things?" (MFM)

Thought that is not reducible to a simple mutilation of actions, but understood as a second way in which actions act.

Thinking is not a minor action, just as action is not a minor thought.

Things are brimming with our feelings. To look at a thing is to take from it the sensations that belong to us and that it had kept (abducted?) for years or minutes. To look at things is to recuperate from them what was ours.

Every glance is individual from beginning to end: you only see what belongs to you; you only look at that which we are. As if the individual human glance always took place in front of a mirror. No one looks, no one sees: I look at me, I see me, and he looks at himself and sees himself.

And with such great perceptual egoism, how can we see things?

We are distracted from things because we exist. To exist, to be alive, is to be distracted from things, beside them: they are lateral to us. They are judged to be banquet or poison, and this alone matters. (What these things are to us, and not, simply: what are these things?)

And thought is inclined not to learning, but to teaching, the role of teacher in relation to the things that surround it. I think about a rock, I am not thought about by it: how can one learn from that which doesn't explain anything?

As if things only had ears and no mouth or thought. As if things were *receiving institutions* and offered up nothing. As if they were orifices where *our* ideas, our shapes take shelter.

Things are holes: *they only learn.*

How, then, do we accept being taught by *nothingness?*, you will say.

"Metaphysical techniques" (MGL)

1—Place a blade beside a glass of water. Grab the blade and dip it in the water three times. Observe closely the results. Put away the blade.

2—Take a religious book and place it in the water in which you just took a bath.
Leave it there until the pages start to come apart.
Let the book deteriorate completely until it disappears in the water.
After patiently waiting for the required amount of time—weeks, perhaps—take a bath in that water, in which the religious book is now included, or dissolved.
Religious water, you murmur. Water with sacred words.

3—Create a sound for every number.

One house on top of another, as if houses were pieces to put together, pieces capable of belonging to something larger: unselfish pieces, incomplete pieces, house-bricks.

"It is the third night of the magnificent night" (MGL)

The night disappears in the middle of the sentence because the sentence was long.

Hours are distributed through space like any other substance.

Rain enters by way of the deceased, flooding the new clothes: black shoes, the deceased is lying upon the ground like things that can be carried.

A living being cannot be carried. It is a different element. Rain falls beside the divine, even, but doesn't touch it. The mystery was calculated so as not to appear. Men with amputated hands clap their hands; pride is glass, easily broken. The heart, an instrument with inexact measurements; the products of love are incorrect—there is no official reference.

Dialogue (3)

Maria Filomena Molder	María Zambrano
"The collector protects treasures, safeguards them, enlarges them"	"The law (common ground where one is with others), the place for everyone, the invisible house that guards the city, where those who are different live."
"The night to be salvaged"	"For the activity of all temples is to dole out the goodness that is contained within them."
"This is not the word, not this one . . . "	"—we have to be seen, the longing to see"
"Place yourself next to that which is always degrading, decomposing, that which always once was."	"And there they are, not crying, just looking, and, while being there just looking, judging."
"The shock of similarity"	"For to be a man is to be fixed in space, is to weigh, to weigh on something else."
" . . . the brevity of our during is no joking matter, even though it is something to laugh at."	" . . . to this religion, which the future has turned into."

Detailed description

The detailed description of chaos fails because there are no details when one does not know the beginning or end of a structure. If the brain is a fragment, where does one start to build?

An erudite declaration of love. Sentimental man who likes libraries. The woman hears, but doesn't understand: What do you mean by this?

The Sun allows light to fall onto a massacre. The bodies reveal the filtration of immobility: the deceased no longer draws near, the corpse lost its capacity to draw near, but even more: the capacity to wait; seven dead maintain a position symmetrical in relation to the bullets they took.
Above the massacre the Sun maintains its expected average velocity. Nature is too large to deal with trifles; your family is a regional occurrence, a minute detail of the planet. An individual cry is practically a secret index.

"we feel movements act" (MFM); movements are things that modify feelings, every movement is sentimental.

Writing as a translation of reading. A translation that is not only incorrect, wrong; more than this: disastrous. I write in an attempt to translate what I have read between two identical languages, but I fail, and thus creativity; invention as an obvious failure, not of repetition but in the attempt to pass something from one side to another. I lost something in the passage, *in transit*, that is: I gained something, because the table that loses one of its four legs during a move from house to another invents, at that very moment, another object with three legs. "I write in full possession of my reading faculties." (MGL)

"The unity that results from subtractions" (MZ)

Diminish what, in the world? Days are not things that can be diminished because they are maintained, as if the following day were a mere repetition of the same day for the last two centuries. Days, plural, are not things that disappear; a day, yes, that one: properly dated.

To date is, then, a way of making something disappear; to give something a date is to hide it. To date is to impede repetition, copy. Everything that is not reproducible has no future, and even the eternal, for example, is not reproducible: there aren't two of it.

"In terms of movement, I went to Sintra, I read Hölderlin" (MGL)

There is, in literature, a movement that begins with a slight tremor/timorousness in the eyes and spreads down to the tips of your feet, which, below the desk, are moving back and forth. There is, in this back and forth movement of the legs of a person who is immobile and reading, an impressive march, *a traversing*: reading is walking.

No place, no country, nowhere is further away than the page I am reading. The page that is twenty centimeters away from my eyes is, ultimately, a much greater distance, depending on my will to perceive it, that is: to perambulate. To perceive something is to perambulate, but at a run, to per-ambulate: to ambulate, running all around it, to perceive a page is to run through every part of the page: we get tired, we've walked too much. "In terms of movement," says MGL, "I went to Sintra, I read Hölderlin."

Reading as a form of physical exercise, reading as a kind of sport: track and field, soccer, gymnastics, reading an essay, handball, figure skating, reading a poem, reading a novel.

To conceive of a gym where the user chooses between aerobics, gymnastics, or reading a work of fiction; each one lasting an hour and a half, three different movement classes.

"The calm race of literature" (MFM)

Every book grants its own speed of reading; like a car, a book should have suggested maximum and minimum speeds for reading on its cover or inside flap: don't read at less than twenty pages an hour, don't read at more than forty pages an hour. (Idea to develop)

Of course speed deceives: imbecilic books, but also perfect books, can be read at high speed, let's say: one hundred pages an hour. It isn't so much the potential speed of reading of a given book that gives it its quality, it is rather the place at which you arrive at that speed.

And what good is it if I am in a car that travels at high speeds, if it arrives at a place where I don't want to be (though quickly, to be sure)?

And what good is it to be in a car that travels at low speeds so that its passengers can appreciate the landscape, if the landscape is not relevant?

Contemplating while traveling if the thing to be contemplated is interesting.

You will say, of course, that reading is good for one's feelings, to fan them: please, don't bring quantitative data into the pleasure of reading.

However, don't forget: what did everyone do with what they read, at the speed at which they read? Landscapes and points of arrival. Economical accounting of reading.

(We cannot read everything. We are mortal, my dear)

"The person who reads cannot look up. To be defenseless..." (MFM)

In wartime, the person who reads will be killed.

War as ostensible enemy of reading; to read (or contemplate) is inadmissible in wartime; it is another variety of treason: the person who reads while others are dying or killing bids farewell sentimentally to their companions, becomes an individual.

You will say: no one can be a reader while their fatherland is being invaded.

Others will say: my fatherland is hardbound: it is a library; that is where I don't feel like a foreigner: amidst all the books. No one can be a reader while the library is being invaded, while it is being burned down. *I don't know how to read ashes,* many readers have already said.

Take note, imagine: a library on fire, the reader's terror. Then: the desperate reader doesn't want to abandon her habits. A woman touches her on the shoulder, asks her to get up: forget the ashes, they aren't paginated.

The ashes mix up the pages to such an extent that they become completely black; the great disorder is the great blackness, the great shapelessness: how can you hold the great disorder?

What do you want to read? The fire has come and gone, your eyes are looking at ashes, and you can pretend that crying is another way for the eyes to read. But it isn't.

"It is in man that we find the elevated ability to produce similarities: his capacity to see similarity is merely an underlying principle of the ancient and powerful coercion to 'become similar and behave as such'" (MFM) apropos of Walter Benjamin.

(collectors) "moved by the hope of finding" (MFM)

It is clear that the collector may or may not be the enemy of the researcher. In truth, the "hope of finding" moves both collector and researcher. Two activities apparently facing opposite directions: facing tomorrow, what does not yet exist (research), and facing yesterday, what already exists (collection).

But to collect is also to research, because to collect is to place two things side by side and to research is also to place two things side by side. (Walter Benjamin, quoted by MFM: "everything that happens is an encounter, a collision.")

Perhaps the difference is: to collect is to place two similar things side by side, and to research is to place two different things side by side. Or better still: apparently alike or apparently different.

Reformulated, then: to collect is to connect things by their similarities, to investigate is to connect things by their differences. The collector is fascinated with similarities, the researcher is fascinated with differences. And if the researcher gives more importance to similarities than to differences, she will enter into a branch of pedagogy: she will be a teacher.

How do things become connected? How do things start to love or hate each other? Cracks in and excess of matter. A crack can also be seen as an excess of matter: I am too empty, there is a zero that wants to press forward, a zero with an appetite.

MFM says: "The disordered order of these chance encounters brings with it the sign of the essential."

Because chance is more important than will or intention. Because intention and will are human; we don't know where chance, on the other hand, comes from. We have, however, a certainty: chance is not human and, below the human, what is there: animals, plants? If we allow this hypothesis we will not be able to take the next step; it is, then, impossible to accept that chance is an effect of an animal or vegetal will. If it is not, then it comes from that which is higher than the human: the divine. "The disordered order of these chance encounters brings with it the sign of the essential."

However, there are no planning meetings for the essential; we've known this for a long time.

Everything that is prepared is pre-pared down, cut to a stop, immobile before it exists. Chance is not; chance pre-moves: before one of these encounters *with* chance happens, chance is already moving somewhere that is not visible. Chance pre-moves; it does not pre-pared down.

"The shock of the similar" (MFM) in the collector.

The shock of perceiving that things love each other.

"Spoken as one who makes up their mind and washes themselves" (MGL)

A sentence doesn't always begin, or a sentence doesn't always start something.

The city, the polis, and in it the man, the politician: that is where the sentence begins. And men understand each other. That is the place—the city—where the sentence starts something, where the sentence has value, where it is considered, heard.

Outside the city, in the forest, and in the city, during moments of great upheaval, the sentence loses its strength; *the sentence starts nothing* and, at last, ceases to exist.

In the city at a moment of chaos: it is action, *now*, that inaugurates everything.

As well as in the forest, or with the madman, or with the fugitive: it is action that starts something.

When intensity is great, when life enters into circuits of absolute commotion, then the sentence can only emerge at the end, after all the actions have been carried out; the sentence only exists as a conclusion (and not as that which does things).

The hero could even be illiterate or mute.

"Method and deviation," writes Walter Benjamin, quoted by MFM.

Method as that which is done after having tripped on something; or: an unplanned, spontaneous movement; so as not to fall after losing balance.

If you touch (put your hands on) a vestige, something, far from there, will feel touched, interrupted in its path, seized upon. Or on the other hand? If you seize upon the vestige, will that from which it originated increase, somewhere, its speed?
The relevant, the premonition: to interfere with vestiges is to interfere with the thing from which it originated.

A writer whose curiosity leaves the page that is in front of her at the moment at which she is writing? The deviated glance deviates. Because the writer is not a reader who, having read the sentence, can deviate her eyes to a non-existent place and stay there for minutes or even hours on end, in immaterial reverie. Much to the contrary, for the writer, reveries should be concrete; materialized to such an extent that they can be placed in plastic bags.
The writer is doing what hasn't been done yet. The reader can put away the book, and the sentence won't escape; the writer *hates the act of putting something away*, because to put away is to not do, and to not do that which hasn't been done yet is a mistake. To not do is the greatest sin.

"Thinking in words" and "acoustic propagation" (MFM) of the poem

The poem is a substance that passes over into the surprises of physics. A verse forges ahead as if it were a thing with electrons and disquietude. It has a nucleus, a positive charge, and a negative charge.

The verse will also have to be a medicine for language, something that brings back the health lost in everyday sentences, in obscenely common commonplaces, the prostituted places in language. A natural medicine, the verse, a salutary element, without side effects; the sickly tongue should receive it with open arms. A space between two words that are habitually connected (a commonplace) allows for the interference, there, in the middle, of another word (or more) that throws the obvious out of balance. For example: instead of commonplace—the common connection of the words *common* and *place*—after opening up space between them (between these two words), one introduces another word, a tiny, not very noisy one. For example: *less*. We are than left with *place-less-common*. A good spot for a word.

And even within a poem there can exist—in this uncommon place—another place-less-common: an intense central verse, which throws it out of balance.

Language cannot be a place of community, of communication in the polis; Language must be the place of the individual, of non-communication, of isolation: *the sentence that isolates me is the sentence that knows me*, it is the sentence that makes me know. Sentences belong to a private place, not a communal one, or else they are not *my* sentences.

To speak always as if one were in the forest, outside the city, without a necessity to communicate, *without the premonition of commerce* which makes words enter into the shared spaces between one man and another, shared commercial spaces: to sell and to buy, we need to find ourselves in a common space, utilizing common words, not individual ones. No one does business with what one does not understand. Understanding in order to do business; removing ambiguity from the sentence.

Sentences that don't emerge from commercial instinct. Sentences that come from the forest.

"With eyes looking forward" (MGL)

It isn't so much a difficulty with the iris or the movement of the pupil; rather, it's about the positioning of will, and there resides the difficulty of movement. It isn't easy to have eyes looking "forward."

To look forward with one's feet. Thus the resolute man.

"with eyes looking forward"—thus another resolute man.

Decisions are, therefore, localized, muscularly, in the feet and eyes.

No one decides anything by internal ratiocinations.
A decision is a visible physiological phenomenon.

"The most delirious and abusive interpretations in the eyes of scientists who have the souls of censors, that is, those who do not theorize with tears in their eyes, as Philo of Alexandria advised (. . .)" (MFM)

Scientists "do not theorize with tears in their eyes"; separation of science/feelings. Emotions are neither techniques nor instruments that are useful in the laboratory; emotion is a remainder and an excess. However, the scientific community craves a science of emotions.

There are no laws governing misfortune or jubilation; laws presuppose a zero emotion, a neutral emotion.

The scientist treats the world as if it were a thing; the scientist transforms her very self into a thing.

In defense, therefore, of emotional theories. *I bring to you, to this conference, a sentimental theory.*

Gilles Deleuze, María Zambrano

A small machine that isn't capable of producing anything except its own image; in front of the mirror, the vainglorious make gestures.

Intense chlorophyll enters into the madman, diminishes the intensity of his movement; introduces a negative intensity—that of plants—a quantity of a *rate of patience*; calmness, like an axe, cuts the log of disquietude. The madman traverses a theory from one end to the other and surrounds himself with *incomplete decisions*.

An incomplete decision is that which establishes action as a decision: indecision becomes a house, a place where one stays put, an indecision that doesn't look around itself, that doesn't know where to go, that has already traversed all other places. It is, therefore, in the center; there are no more hypotheses: it remains.

Inspiration is the result of the fear that memory occupies thought completely; I don't want to be captured by the past, I make an effort: I inspire myself.

Inspiration as a manifestation of the future: the future arrived; I did something that I didn't know I was capable of doing.

Decadence can climb stairs; it will not get younger, it will not, ultimately, cease to fall, to descend.

(Living is adultery committed behind death's back; without it knowing, retreating from it: one lives.)

"The necessity to speak endlessly is one of the luxuries—one of the wastes—of the civilized. Life in the city is what unleashes this endless speech" (MZ)

When one is not afraid, one can speak. The vocabulary emerged in its entirety during moments of safety; when faced with a threatening enemy, man is mute and physically agile. The urgency of movement and the patience of discourse.

Words exist because waiting exists: the before. And also: the after.

In order to tell the story of actions that have already taken place, words emerge. Before and after. Not during. A man engaged in movement in the present is mute. But he is afraid.

"In every face there is something that only someone else (and not just any someone) can discover and mold: we all have our parents, our children, those we love, those we obey." (MFM)

You do not consume the strength of another by looking at him at length, but ultimately, yes: you consume the strength of the other by looking at him at length. Don't do this if you don't love him.

Those you obey; how do you obey? It's interesting to think of the inventor-man as someone who simply obeys orders: now, invent! An exotic slave: he carries out an order the way a novelty is carried out, like someone who made something new appear before the eyes of someone who requested it.

How can you surprise the person who made the order, bringing into being exactly what was ordered, without error?

Look at nature. That is the answer.

The face as a thing that is touched, that is: a thing perfectible from the outside; a stone with a nervous system: thus the face.

Because the face has a contract with the nervous impressions of the organism; smiling is not an external action, it is a biological fact that traverses and perturbs the doubly dense and doubly invisible flesh.

And look closely at this expression; discover the details, investigate it: *doubly invisible*.

How can it be doubly invisible?

How can you quantify, subdivide, multiply something that is singular?

Because it isn't happening or hasn't yet happened or already happened. To be strong is to be unable to be looked at while one is strong. That which is strong has no path it takes, has no center: it appears and disappears. Nor doesn't even have the *and* that can give the illusion of connection between two facts or two moments. On the contrary, that which is strong appears-disappears (in a single word, a new word: that which appears is that which disappears at the same instant); appears-disappears.

Doubly invisible, this is a heresy.

"There is no word that only knows itself, every word carries within itself, transports an incessant pursuit of all other words, digging down, descending ever deeper, like a poor miner" (MFM)

The science of pursuit requires apprenticeship, unlike the science of being pursued. Fleeing is natural, pursuit requires technique, a nose for clues, alternative speeds; one who pursues is not alone: provides answers; one who is pursued is alone: asks questions, causes confusion.

However, it is the case that the most effective pursuer modifies the quality of these two professions and does not pursue by running after, he pursues by surprising, manifesting himself as an element that can introduce the new. A pursuer who places false clues in the path of the pursued, breaking the ancient connection between hunter and hunted.

The pursued belongs to the category of that which *appeared first*, the pursuer is that which *came later*. The pursued who arrives late, who comes later than the pursuer, would be a paradox.

How long ago did my pursuer pass through here?—asks the fugitive, gasping for breath.

"Movement of placing fact into the pains of difficulty" (MFM)

The fact, thrust from the invisible, resides in a place where night is not sufficient to impede vision. The fact interrupts a greater poetry. From the other side, the invisible, there are neither markets nor trumpets: the noise is a lateral mode of something being explicit, another mode of exhibiting length, width, and volume: sound occupies space.

A plane put into the sky as litter. A child closes her eyes, not in order to not see, but in order to clean. However, there is still the noise of the machine: the abundant mechanisms of disruption of the minimal, the infiltration of the decadent in the recently-appeared; machines do not swear oaths in the open air; repeating—the way machines do—isn't fulfilling an oath, it is the impossibility of invention.

Take note: machines do not mature, they do not acquire wisdom; it wouldn't make sense to attribute the word wisdom to any place close to the word machine. It doesn't *know*, it just *does*.

A machine does not forget, and that which could be a target of praise must also be the origin of a fear: how to be safe next to something that does not forget?

A landscape with a fly in it will become a singular landscape when, recovered from the surprise of the appearance of the insect, we forget about it, as much at the level of the visual as at the level of the auditory—and that which is forgotten is landscape.

Nine clouds above a bicycle prepare rain. A bicycle at rest, motionless, fallen to the earth like a dog that has taken a bullet right in the biological location of its survival. A child tied a shoe near the back wheel, then ran off; an adult man lifted up the bicycle by its straps, as if that instrument of movement also had shoulders. He lifted the bicycle off the ground like a son lifts his elderly mother out of bed. But there was a shoe on it. A disturbing shoe connected to the primitive walking machine. The adult pushes the bicycle, and the shoe, connected to the brake cable, follows behind the rear wheel, walking as if it were useful. But this mad caravan of an adult man, a bicycle, and the shoe following them like a detective, and the nine dark and aroused clouds, ready to disappear out of love for the liquid state, this caravan of mistaken admixtures interrupts an astute man who, at his collector's table, is separating adverbs from nouns with logical tweezers and an athlete's stamina.

The mental operations of the nervous system are startled by details of reality that are not collectible, that cannot be placed one beside the other. Individual details, because of their individuality, become unparalleled divinities, things without a left or right side, without lovers or elements that domesticate them. No one knows where that which is unique and new comes from. How can we await that which will soon bring us astonishment? It is impossible to await astonishment, you will say.

Brief Notes on Music

Testers

Thinking about music testers similar to wine testers. They test with their ear: thirty seconds of sound and they quickly perceive the essential.

Seven orchestras in seven different rooms, closed rooms. The sound tester opens, one after the other, each of the doors and tilts his auditory system in the direction of the sound for thirty seconds. During thirty seconds of life, nothing exists except for thirty seconds of music. Or rather, they are not thirty seconds of life, they are thirty seconds of music. That's it. The tester moves on to the next room. When finished, he says: I choose that room, that music.

Definition of Music

It's clear that the expression "long ears" doesn't result merely from an anatomical description. *Long ears* are those who know how to hear.

In ancient China, men with "long ears" were considered wise, and the Taoists speak of the capacity, which some men possess, to receive an "auricular light." This is also a beautiful definition of music.

The Melomaniac-Physiognomist

Attempting to perceive music through the face of the person listening to it.

Let's imagine a man, a melomaniac-physiognomist, who has his ears covered and doesn't have any information about the concert program. He even has his back to the orchestra, facing the other spectators.

The melomaniac-physiognomist tries to concentrate on the faces of the audience members at the concert. On the manner in which one or another member of the public furrows her brow and even the way one or another taps her knee, subtly, with the fingers of her right hand.

However, above all, he fixates on the faces of those who are listening to what he cannot hear. And, yes, an eminent specialist in music and human nature will be able to say, with certainty, from the observation of the physiognomy of the listeners: Mozart! Bach! Chopin! And perhaps even this: Silence.

Music and Matter

Thinking about a piece of music can change the color of things. Not in a poetic manner, but a concrete, pragmatic way. Or rather, just as the Sun, with its intense light, hits against the exterior wall of a building and, after a few months, the color of the wall starts to change—strong colors start to lose their strength, a vivid yellow starts to become a faint yellow—we can also imagine that music, sounds, could do the same.

Imagine, then, an orchestra that, having played repeatedly in a room, starts to change the color of the interior walls, but with results that are inverse to those of exposure to the light of the Sun. Imagine a piece of music capable, over time, of transforming a pale yellow into a vivid yellow.

We could even imagine that different types of music would be able to alter the color of the walls in different ways.

Music capable of interfering with matter, that is what is sought.

Death and Music

Mead was a drink that some traditions associated with immortality.
Another method of guaranteeing immortality might be good listening, good hearing. As if a piece of music could transform into a message, a secret that allows a mortal to live a little while longer. This, then, is what is quickly put into place in an imaginary country: an itinerant orchestra made up of musician-medics try to find the piece of music that will not save the person who is about to die, but that will at least postpone death for a little while.
Death respects nothing, as is well known. It emerges, ill-mannered, in any part of the world and at any time, but we can believe that, if a group of musicians find the right melody to calm a dying person, death will, at least, wait a while so as not to interrupt.
But beware, of course, because the slightest pause, the merest wrong note and death will enter.

Music and the Equilibrium of Elements

It has been long known: music is one of the quickest ways to agitate human physiology. It rivals amorous connection and desire.

Ancient Chinese masters, for example, divided up notes into half-tones and made each half tone correspond with a psychological sensation.

Music is a potential of chemical reactions; a form of immediate contagion. The sadness or joy of a piece of music is passed on to those who listen.

Deep down, we have two entities, two substances: the person who listens and the music. And what occurs is a sort of osmosis at the level of these large particles called human beings. There is a transit of elements from one side to the other, in an attempt to attain an equilibrium of the whole. And thus, then, at the end of a piece of music, it almost seems that the music has become less sad and the listener more so. The listener and the music transform into a single element.

Music is absorbed the way that something that is in the air and unseen is absorbed. It is, in fact, a substance—and that sonorous substance can have a sad, joyous, neutral, melancholic, or stimulating charge. And substances capable of provoking such distinct reactions are rare in this world.

Music and Temperature

For example, can music dry what is wet? Alter the physical state of things? Transform ice into water, water into ice?

Can music produce effects similar to those produced by the heat or cold?

Designating pieces of music as cold or hot should have concrete consequences. A piece of music that warms or cools the environment—shouldn't such a change be registered by a scientific and objective thermometer?

Labyrinth and Sound

Sound, we should note, is always an energy that travels a labyrinthine route.

The human ear is made to hear music, and it isn't by chance that its internal structure isn't a straight line, much to the contrary: it is curved and counter-curved, counter-curved and curved.

And, in the labyrinth, this strange thing occurs: moving forward is often the same as moving backwards.

I am in a labyrinth.

I move forward, or rather: I retreat.

And sometimes: I retreat, or rather: I move forward.

And this is a possible definition of music. I move forward, or rather: I retreat. I retreat, or rather: I move forward.

The Tranquil Listener

The manner of delaying the world's onward march forward can be called labyrinth.
The labyrinth, however, as the geometric—and psychological—inverse of the straight line.
The shortest distance between two points: the straight line.
The longest distance between two points: the labyrinth.
Therefore: the labyrinth as the anatomical enemy of the straight line.
And the human ear, let's return to it, possesses a labyrinth instead of a straight line.
The labyrinth, delaying that which comes from the outside, gives the brain time to prepare for the arrival of sound. The labyrinth of the ear is a symbolic form of preparation and digestion.
And thus, then, two possible ways of listening to music: the listener who listens in a straight line and the listener who hears by respecting the shape, with its many curves, of the ear. This is the patient, unhurried listener. The other is deaf.

A Project

1.
A man who liked to listen to music in the dark, but with a flashlight in his hand.

When he turned on the flashlight, he didn't point it towards the technological apparatus from which the sounds emerged, but instead the space towards which the music flowed. He wanted to locate the sounds the way one locates an object.

2.
Deep down, that man wanted what many have attempted for over centuries: to locate, with the aid of light, the position of sound.

But the sensation that one has in a room is different from what Physics teaches us. The sensation felt by that man was that the light from the flashlight always got there too late: the sound had already passed through there and was now somewhere else. With the flashlight it was clear: the sound was always further ahead.

Sonorous Morality

Tell me where you are looking, and I will tell you what your morality is. Well sure, but morality also depends on the proper utilization of one's hearing. Tell me what you are listening to, and I will tell you the weight of your guilt. What sentences you hear, what sentences you pay attention to. What music you listen to, what music you pay attention to.

Listening is a subtle form of turning our body to one side. If I hear a sound that is coming in my direction, even if I don't turn my body towards it, it is already mentally directed to my right side. That.

We could say: if someone speaks very loudly at my right side and, at the same time, another person speaks very softly at my left side, I am obligated to hear more on my right side. We could say this, indeed, but perhaps it isn't true. The fact is that if you were to give it more attention, you would be able to hear the sound that is at a lower exterior volume. Deciding what sound to pay attention to is, ultimately, deciding at what volume you will set the different parts of the world. It's an important decision.

Decision and Two Types of Volume

We could thus think that there are two types of volume—the external volume of the sound, easily measurable with well-known apparatuses, and, further, the internal volume of the sound. Paying attention to one side or paying attention to the opposite side is the way for mortal humans to decide on the volume of sounds in the world.

Because listening is a choice, it is a decision, not a passive occurrence. Sometimes we are in a place and, without wanting to, we hear something. However, being in a place where determined subjects are spoken of is already the result of a decision (to have decided to go to that locale). Having gone *there*, I have decided to hear what is normally heard *there*, in that place.

Ninety percent of what we hear is, therefore, the result of a pragmatic decision: I want to hear this.

Someone who decides that she wants to hear classical music walks over to a recording or a concert hall (at the appropriate hour).

Someone who decides that she wants to hear a concrete mixer in operation walks to a construction site and concentrates on listening to the mild noise of the concrete mixer.

What we hear is also, then, a decision made by our legs. Where do you go? And what do you want to hear?—the same question formulated in two different ways.

On Difficult Music (a)

Suddenly, this: music issues forth and we cannot identify it. It isn't just not knowing the name of the composer or the date of the work: it's not knowing what path the notes are taking (or even, sometimes: what notes are these?). Not recognizing a piece of music, being lost when confronted by a piece of music. The sounds aren't reaching me; they get lost.

In a literary context, an author speaks of "mapping the forest," and that's where we are: how do we know the way in the middle of a dense forest? How do we distinguish what has already by seen from what hasn't yet been seen when we're in the middle of a dense forest, a thick, uniform forest, the same over here as it is over there, over there and over here?

The dense forest is that which does not allow space for a human body to advance. The dense forest expels humans. The dense, uniform forest with branches and branches and not even a square meter of empty space, the dense forest says: through here you shall not advance. And the human comes to a stop.

The dense forest is also this: you cannot see beyond the trees that surround you. Because empty space is necessary for you to see far.

And a dense forest of sounds is also this: it doesn't provide me a path, I cannot advance.

Difficult music? Forest. But the good listener wants to open up a powerful clearing within it.

On Difficult Music (b)

Difficult music as a dense and uniform forest.

But this is always there when one listens and when one tries to see. We try to make maps of the forest, even; even of the sounds of the forest—that's what we call non-domestic sounds, sounds that our ear cannot identify—we even try to create a city from the sounds of the forest. Urbanizing what we do not understand, that is one of the tasks, one of the instincts of humans.

And it's this: we are dealing with urbanizing what is not understood, that which lacks order, which does not have primary or secondary routes, since all paths are identical. To urbanize: to construct routes for men and their families.

And this is also a definition of what it is to be lost: all paths are identical.

And we are, then, faced with another strange, paradoxical, and extreme form of nihilism, of desistance: being lost, which is nihilism by incompetence: it being all the same if we turn to the left or to the right because we don't know where we are. It's all the same, in short, not because of moral or willful motives, but out of simple spatial disorientation.

I am indifferent about where I will go, not because I'm philosophically disoriented, I am indifferent about where I will go because I'm geographically disoriented.

A Hot-Air Balloon above the City Center

Above the noise of chaotic traffic, a hot-air balloon. (The hot-air balloon was invented in 1783 by two paper manufacturers. At bottom, it is this: a sack of paper that flies, that's the hot-air balloon.)

Ok then, a maestro is up there, alone, in the balloon, and the movements he makes could be directed at the birds or the clouds, who knows?

But now we see it better: the maestro is not facing up, but facing down. In essence, what he is doing is calming the earth—or at least this is perhaps what he is attempting to do.

The maestro believes that the precise and elegant movements of his baton, when performed far from the musicians, have a different effect. That maestro believes that these movements are a manual, artisanal, and ancient way to calm the storms of the sea and the quaking of the earth.

But the maestro is up above a city, at its center, and for that reason there is neither sea nor empty earth to be calmed.

And now, indeed, we perceive what the maestro is doing moving his baton way up there in the hot-air balloon—and we perceive its effects. What he is doing is directing the traffic.

What appeared to be the normal movements for conducting an orchestra are, ultimately, movements of the wrist indicating directions for the cars: to the right, to the left—as well as speeds: now slower, now faster.

And thus it is, then, that down below the maestro's hot-air balloon, an astonishing thing occurs: the traffic, as if by a miracle, seems to finally, after many years, calm down. Cars swerve out of the way of each other, at the last minute, and there isn't a single accident, a single honking of a horn—as if in an incredibly synchronized ballet. Each car knows when to proceed and when to stop, when to accelerate and when to ease up. Like a musician. What melody accompanies the cars today?—this is a common question now, in that harmonious city.

The Geometrician-Listener

What do we do when shapeless music reaches our ear, with melodies that make us tipsy, that make us dizzy, that makes us fall down, that make us ask for a chair to sit in? This is what we do: we desist and say: it's not music, it's noise. Or, instead, we try to give a shape to this shapelessness/misshapenness. We try to trace squares onto what is chaotic, trace triangles, rectangles, and circumferences onto what appears to have more than a thousand sides.

Thus the attentive ear: it is, more than anything else, a geometrician-ear. An ear that tries to organize sounds into shapes. (To traverse from a modality of time to a modality of space.)

Noise is, then, that for which the geometrician-listener still has not found a pencil capable of making decisive strokes. Strokes that define the interior and the exterior, the right side and the left, bottom and top. Organizing strokes.

Because the geometrician-listener does this: draws on top of the sounds; draws with the ear, such a strange action; draws with her attention, with her meticulous hearing, draws by separating, organizing—drawing an insane sound closer to other sounds that can aid in its comprehension.

An insane sound that is rescued by a family of sensible sounds, this is the tranquil utopia of the listener faced with sonorous clamor. Even to you, sound that I cannot understand, shall I end up giving a name!

The Doctor-Listener

How is it that a sound ceases to be insane, how is it that a sound ceases to be delirious? Precisely the way that a person ceases to be insane. When something or someone understands it, listens to it, and says, in a clear, sincere manner: I understand you. Understanding the person or thing that is insane is to have already cured it, to have already ceased to consider it insane.

Why not think, then, of the good listener as a person who, faced with chaotic sound, acts like a doctor, calming the sound, mastering the instability with that ancient form of mastering that is to classify, to categorize?

I am here—the doctor-listener might say—I am here to cure sounds, to restore the health of sounds, to understand, first of all, the sounds that others call insane or misshapen. I am here to listen to the insane sound, and after listening to it a lot, I'm certain that I will understand it. This, then, is the listener-physician, the physician-listener: she restores the health of the music, but not by introducing something into its body/organism, it restores the health of the music with the opposite attitude—that of waiting, or an attempt at comprehension. I cured you because I listened to you. I cured you because I paid attention to you. I turned you into music (you, who were merely noise) because, instead of insulting you, I sat down and tried to compare my library of sounds with the sounds that you presented to me. And I inaugurated a space.

The Orchestra at High Altitudes

An orchestra that plays at the top of the highest mountain.
Difficulties breathing first interfere with the men who play wind instruments, of course, but another method of bodily oxygenation goes from the lungs to the extremities: legs begin to shake, hands get tired.

The orchestra did not prepare for physical exercise at high altitude. There it is, therefore, with less strength every passing minute, slowing down the music. Each note is now shambolically wrested from the sheet music, like an athlete who is only able to run like a child.

And suddenly we realize that sheet music should be adapted for high altitude—slower, drawn-out notes.

And, yes, after five minutes—at an altitude of two thousand meters—all of the tempos are drawn out for the orchestra, not out of the expressive intention of the music, but out of the will of the atmosphere, the oxygen, the difficulty breathing.

Impossible to play *prestissimo* or *vivacissimo*. The sensation is really that the fast tempo of a piece of music would interfere with things that exist high above the earth—with some heavenly bodies, perhaps, at most; definitely in the flight paths of birds and one or another satellite.

And thus at the top of the mountain, we see a plaque, next to others that indicate the danger of falling and suggest a thousand precautionary measures. Up there, then, is the plaque, at an altitude of two thousand meters: beware fast tempos.

Sheet music adapted to atmospheric conditions: to be played at sea level, music to be played at an altitude of two thousand meters, music to be played under the sea, music to be played near fire and volcanoes.

An Imaginary Excavation

And he was a clearheaded man, but said this: sometimes we excavate and undertake, underneath our feet and by force of shovel and our own muscles, to unearth a church, from which emerges, for example, a sound or various sounds.

In fact, we can imagine this situation in our head: conducted by a musician-archeologist, an archeologist-musician, a thousand men began to dig into the earth in search of a sound. In search, therefore, of anything that lacks width, length, and height. Men who dig not to find ancient relics, treasures, or bones that explain the extinction of dinosaurs—but who dig simply to try to find a song.

Take note, however, that this is not about wanting to locate sheet music or the ancestors of sheet music. What they want to find, these hallucinating excavators, are the sounds themselves. A thousand men in a valley in Egypt searching for songs that the ancients whistled. That is the fossil they all desire, the rarest one, the one that preserves what the ancients sang and whistled. Acoustic fossils, for these searches the melomaniac-archeologist, whose head, like a Don Quixote of music, was enchanted, not by the chivalric romances he read, but by the excess of music he listened to. And a thousand men continue to dig, believing in this new Quixote. "Dig more," demands the musician-archeologist-hallucinator, "I feel like we are about to discover an ancient sound. One last push, please, one last push!"

On Musical Fossils

Indeed, we know what they drew, what they painted; we know the objects they used, we know where they lived and how—but what do we know of the songs they played or sang? The fact is we have lost the songs, the music of the ancients. Or were they mute—a human species that did everything with its hands and eyes, and nothing with its vocal cords?

The prehistory of mankind seems mute; or at least we have turned our ancient parents into mutes with hands and a brain. Hands and brain used in battle against other predators and against other beings, apparently docile ones who are nevertheless not thought of as capable of producing music. If I have two hands that are quite free in space, if I am a biped and take pride in this, well, I ask myself: what did my ancestor-hands do aside from immediately useful things? What history tells us is that they made objects, fire, refined utensils, they killed, strangled, slaughtered and, every once in a while, saved a life. But the hands of the ancients also painted and drew and, yes, of course, touched the world that existed so that the world that existed, in contact with the surfaces of their bodies, would produce music. But of this we know very little. We know of some instruments, but not the music. We've recovered the skeleton, but not the blood.

An Excessive Definition, but a Definition

Henri Jeanson once said that an opera singer "is a person who takes a knife in the back and, instead of bleeding, sets about singing."

Taking out the sarcasm, this is the operation that is described (on the stage all is possible): managing to represent pain in a beautiful manner.

The Order of Sounds

It's just like with language: sentences said from back to front confound the reader, put her in an intermediate time, suspended between understanding and not understanding. Manuals of classical psychology suggest that between these two sentences or phrases
The dog chases the cat
and
The cat is chased by the dog
there is a difference, but not a difference in the action proper. In these two phrases, the dog and the cat do the same things, but, for the reader, the second phrase takes more time to be understood (sometimes, understanding a sentence and being able to see the actions that are recounted by it are the same thing).

In fact, there is a narrative in phrases; in the shortest of phrases there is still a *Once upon a time*. Someone does something. Well then, that's a story. And the story that exists in a phrase, even in the shortest ones, ends with a full stop (and not necessarily with the princess marrying the prince).

And if we think about *sonorous phrases*, we see that they also have a beginning, middle, and end, even if they are in a different order. It was Lewis Carroll who said: begin at the beginning, go on till you come to the end, then stop—sensible advice, which not all musicians follow. Starting at the middle: this is a possibility, for example, that all the arts, across all eras, have utilized with great frequency.

And there are also, then, songs that come to us as if from back to front, songs in which we do not immediately understand where the subject and predicate are—who does what? What sound does what?

We can, therefore, say that in classical music:

The dog chases the cat

while in avant-garde music, completely innovative, three hundred years later, what happens is something radically different: The cat is chased by the dog.

Sounds that Save, Sounds that Make you Dance

1.
It is truly a shame that we don't know what the first *homo sapiens* sang.

2.
It is inconceivable that the brain did not, for millennia, steer its capabilities towards making playful sounds, useless sounds.

Because we have no doubts—there are two fundamental sounds, from the beginning of the world:

1—the cry for help (the sound that requests help).

2—the threatening cry (the sound that says: I can kill you!).

There are also other sounds that are variants, or lower in the hierarchy (so to speak), yet still connected to these two fundamental sounds, to these two sounds of survival.

For example, there are

—sounds that make friends retreat from a more powerful enemy

and

—sounds that call friends to come devour a weaker enemy.

Two variations of the cry for help and the threatening cry.

3.

And apart from this, from these sounds of survival, what did our ancestors do with music?

We can imagine that, after devouring the enemy, at long last without threats and no longer hungry, the human voice was able to make non-utilitarian sounds, and hands could cease to make precise gestures aimed towards an objective, and feet could stop running in effective and precise manner; and hands and feet were finally able, at that moment, surrounding the same spot and same surfaces of the earth, to produce sounds that made their friends dance. Thus, music, its origin. No threat, no hunger.

For a few moments, the man at the foot of his friend can make sounds that are not directed towards retreat or attack, sounds that are not made for killing or rescuing. What a relief!

Mathematics that Make Noise (Music)

Mathematics that leap and fall; sonorous mathematics. Learning to count on your hands, learning to count by Do Re Mi. Two forms of initiation into calculus, two forms of exercising the head.

Music and Ratiocination

Repeatedly whistling a melody is to name a way of thinking. A way of thinking that is fixed: that is the whistled melody. Whistling as a sonorous way of presenting an axiom. A habitual piece of music transforms into a habitual ratiocination.

Drawing, Language, Mathematics, Music

A woman walks toward a street on which is written: 2+2=4.
On another street the sentence: THIS IS THE STREET OF LANGUAGE.
On another street, also on the ground, a drawing.
On another street, also on the ground: nothing. But in the air, something. A sound.

Neighbors and Thought

1.
A form of not being alone: you sing. Another ancient form is this: you think.

2.
Singing is a sonorous form of not being alone.
Thinking is a mute form of not being alone.
If you have neighbors with sensitive and ill-humored ears: you think.
If you have good neighbors: you sing.

3.
And, in a certain way, these are two actions with two opposite directions. If you sing, something moves from the inside to the outside (the sound?).
If you think, something goes from the outside to the inside, or from the inside to the inside, or from the inside to another inside in some other part of the brain. Definitively: you do not think to the outside, you do not think from the inside out.

4.
Can you think while you sing? Is it possible to sing and think at the same time? Is it possible to whistle and think at the same time; play piano and think at the same time? At the precise moment of a Do Re Mi, to ponder a philosophical thesis?

Of course one possible exaggeration is this: if we don't want others to think, we force them to sing.

Don't think right now: sing.

But of course things are not that simple.

Description

Sometimes sounds demand that you stand up, other times that you sit down.
Sometimes there is a sort of war between sounds, other times there is a game.
Sometimes that which seems random, other times the aiming of an arrow at the center of the target.

Decisions and Music

We know quite well that while we are swimming we can think, quite a bit even—and it is while we are out for a swim that, sometimes, we make the most significant decisions for that existence which exists outside of the water, on solid ground. (It is when you pretend to be a fish or amphibian that you decide what is best for you as a mammal with feet quite firmly on the ground.)

We can imagine a musician who makes his big decisions not before or after playing, but during the exact moment of the performance; at the moment when she concentrates completely on her instrument and on the melody, that is when she makes the most important decision. I play in order to decide what to do with the rest of my life, this musician might say.

Imagine, then, a fictional character: a man who is incapable of making decisions unless he is at the piano, playing; and imagine other characters incapable of making decisions without playing a certain piece of music, a certain clarinet or saxophone.

While I play, I do not think, but I do make decisions—someone might say.

This is not, however, about thinking while playing, this is about directing the body to a physical state that demands a decision be made.

If you take your body to the crossroads, the next step will be a decision: if you go to the left, you will not go to the right. So much is obvious; this is what the decision imposes upon you. The musician, then, as someone whose music takes her not to the crossroads, but straight to the decision made, to the path chosen.

Making the most important decisions about existence at the exact moment when one is thinking about something else.

When I hesitate, when I don't know what to do, I start to play. When I have finished playing, I have already made my decision, says the musician.

The Oldest Melody

An ethologist, Irenäus Eibl-Eibesfeldt, refers to the studies of F. Sauer, who "raised blackcap birds in isolation from each other and isolated from any noise."

Birds artificially placed into a mute world—into a world that neither speaks nor sings. And in that mute world, it is if the birds have been rendered deaf. If there is no one who sings or plays an instrument, then why should someone who can hear even exist?

Well, the relevant part of this experiment was to verify that, despite being raised in an environment devoid of the sounds of their fathers, mothers, siblings, friends, and enemies, these birds grew up and acquired a song similar to that of their species—"the information relative to the type of model melody is contained in the genetic material," concluded the ethologist.

A bird sings the melody that its genes already know; it sings the melody of the great-grandparents it never knew. It doesn't learn it in a school, nor does it imitate anyone else.

In some way, it is the cells that sing; we are confronted with a singing physiology, a physiology that already possesses a melody, already has sheet music; an individual physiology that exists as if it were already destined to be a part of an orchestra; when you combine this physiology with other birds, what results is, at heart, a natural orchestra: musicians who instinctively play the same tune, without rehearsal.

Imagine this, then: babies who grow up to sing, for example, some of Mozart's beautiful melodies without ever having heard them before. Just as the blackcaps don't need to hear the song of their species in order to sing it, something similar could occur with humankind. A Mozart melody that is already inscribed in our genes.

But this is perhaps what makes man an animal that is, despite all else, worthy of admiration: perhaps every one of us has a melody inscribed in our genes—or more than one—but, if we indeed have one, this melody would certainly be individual to us. Every person would have their own ancestral song—a song that doesn't need to be heard in order to be sung.

The First and Last Song

This is, perhaps, a characteristic of our species: our genes preserve certain familial melodies—those of our most ancient family; melodies that, without study or imitation, we recall from ancestral times. A melody that comes to us through our instincts—this is what someone who is born first sings (might crying ultimately be a troubled and ancient form of song?); and then, on the other hand, those who receive the ones who have just been born (father, mother), already know how to hear and interpret this song. The listener also has an ancient ear.

And perhaps there are even those other men who, at a certain point during their lives, are able to find within themselves that ancestral music, and likely only in their final moments, in bed, at death's door, does that melody appear. And, yes, if we hear a dying person humming an unknown tune, we can be certain that they are, at that moment, revealing the instinct of those birds who know a song that they've never learned: thus it is, then, that on the bed of the moribund the oldest melody of the oldest ancestors appears. And this might be, perhaps, a sensible way for the body to bid farewell to its days.

Two Forms of Being Sound

Sedentary music and nomadic music.

Music that has a house, that returns at the end of the day to the room it recognizes, to its family members.

And music that has an erratic route; music that wanders, therefore, and takes the wrong way back; music that gets lost, that ends up at a point very different from the point where it started.

Take note here: there are two very different reasons for being far from the roof of one's shelter. The first: not knowing the way back home; and the second: not wanting to return home. Incompetence or desire.

1—Sedentary music: domestic; 2—nomadic music: doesn't have a home, doesn't have a family (aside from that which follows its steps, accompanies its wanderings).

Two forms of music: sedentary and nomadic. I go forth because I want to return. Or: I go forth because I don't want to return. And I always go forth, either way.

How to Comment on a Song (1)

1.
One does not debate a song. Or does one debate a song?

Argument and counter-argument are apparently not valid in the face of a sound that does not speak, in the face of a sound that does not exhibit the logical trajectory of a language.

However, there is, here and there—and more there than here—verbal commentary about music, about a piece of music. One who hears sounds argues with words, and another person, another listener, counter-argues with other words. Words, words, words. They debate and comment on a song that never even said "ah," that never said a "yes" or a "no."

A strange thing, then. But how does one do it? Commenting on a piece of music by going to over to the piano, picking up a cello? Commenting on a piece of music by playing another piece, commenting through a combination of notes?

2.
Music is, in a certain manner, mute when it comes to language. Sounds do not speak, they exist as a physical element that appears one moment and immediately disappears—like a stone that existed, occupied space, and had mass, but only for a microsecond—and soon thereafter disappearing.

An ephemeral stone, that is sound; a momentary stone, that is sound. And this is strange, of course.

And sheet music (for those able to read it) can be viewed, then, as the announcement of this ephemeral stone, a threat that it will appear.

But yes, music is this: its manner of appearing is the same as its manner of disappearing.

How to Comment on a Song (2)

Saying, of a song you hear, simply: *I like it* or *I don't like it* is already to confront what is heard with a verb. The verb, the word, as that which attempts to force something that exists solely in that strange world of the ears (and their internal connections) to descend into the world of men.

Of course, a person who hears a song can respond to the sound in an animalistic manner. Facial expressions of pleasure or displeasure, twisting of the body, internal ways that viscera instinctually respond to what they hear. Very well, these are some examples of organic forms of reacting to sound. However, when the listener stands up and, instead of remaining mute, says: *I liked it*, he enters onto a different plane. The animal that listens transforms into a man who speaks. A short while ago I listened as a living and organic being, now I am speaking and commenting on what I listened to, as a thinking being. While you listen, you do not think, you concentrate on the sounds—someone might say. After the song is over, then, yes, you think about what you've heard. Reflecting on sounds is, then, a strange activity. It's like verbally commenting on an equation, a mathematical formula; or drawing a picture of a song—a drawing that explains the song.

And we can think of a movement like this: we perceive mathematics through drawings, we perceive drawings through words, we perceive words through numbers, we perceive music through mathematics and geometry, and so on and so forth. We perceive a certain world with the instruments of another world.

Perhaps this comparison is excessive, but wouldn't this be the same as trying to learn Chinese by studying Italian?

At any rate, speaking after listening to a symphony is, nevertheless, one of the best responses of the human organism. It's better, despite all this, than merely furrowing one's brow.

Sound, Precision, and God

Mathematics are not made to be sung, but we can imagine an orchestra in which every one of its elements puzzles through an equation. In which the singing or the sound of an instrument are similar to the trajectory of mathematics when one attempts to solve a difficult problem. In which the sound is a form, a trajectory, by which one moves from the complex to the simple, from great confusion to the only number capable of solving and pacifying. Music as a ratiocination that starts with the first sound, which is the problem, and arrives at the end of the song and brings into existence the final sound, the one that solves the problem.

But there are songs in which the end does not bring it to an end, but to a beginning; in which the end is, therefore, a threat or an expectation, in which the end does not suggest satisfied passivity, but demands, on the contrary, that the listener stand up, because her muscles and reason require action.

Steiner recalls a mysterious phrase from Leibniz "when he sings to himself, God sings algebra," Leibniz, who associated language with "audible reason," reason that makes itself heard; reason, therefore, that occupies the space between the mouth that speaks and the ear that listens. Reason become sound: we speak to others, we listen to others.

But then how can there be so much mystery in song when at times it is so precise?

Mysterious reason that turns into sound—this is, perhaps, a definition of the music that enchants us the most.

Whether God sings a precise song, whether God sings the precise; or whether God, on the contrary, sings confusion, ambiguity, the unresolved?—this is the question that can be posed.

Does God sing cryptic verses or does God sing the infallible resolution of a long equation?

"My dear," some will say, "it's always preferable to understand."

"My dear," others will say, "despite it all, despite it all, it's preferable not to understand, not to understand, not to understand."

Intention and Music

Sometimes this is perceived: music transformed into a tool; into the "hammer" of Pavlov. If you wish to create tension: use this song; if you wish to show that a bad man is coming: use this song. For the good man: this song; for men and women madly in love: use this song. To make the gentleman listener afraid: song A; to calm the gentleman listener: song B.

Sounds, then, as elements that announce certain images. This is very clear, for example, in the use of music in television.

Music, therefore, transformed into a method for attaining a sensation. Music that knows very well what it wants; obvious music, which does not hesitate; music that works toward objectives, like the most contemporary and efficient managers; hammer-music, screwdriver-music, music that possesses an objective, task-music; music that does this, music that does that.

Eyes Closed Tightly

Two ways of listening to music: opening one's eyes, closing one's eyes.

There is also a third option: listening to music with eyes closed tightly. This might seem overly precious, but it isn't. In truth, there aren't merely two options. Eyes can be slightly or tightly closed.

Eyes that are closed mean that they are not distracted by any external image. And this is good.

Eyes that are closed tightly mean that they are neither distracted by any external image (they are closed) nor by any internal image or recollection (they are closed tightly).

There are, therefore, listeners with eyes open, with eyes closed, and with eyes closed tightly.

Should the price of tickets for a concert be the same for these three listeners?

Never Listen Back

The superstition of never looking back, that biblical curse, is well known. But this is seldom spoken of: never listening back. This, on the other hand, would be foolish advice, because ancient music is, ultimately, a way of elucidating future steps, this much seems evident. Turning your head back to listen is, from a certain point of view, to respect the past.

And we can imagine a character who faces the future in orthodox manner, the only path, he says. I never look back, I never listen back. In musical terms, it is the following: this character, a man who is enormously falling into the future (a temporal fall), never listens to a song that he has heard before; new music every day, that is what he demands.

Let's say that he also doesn't want to smell anything he has smelled before, not touch what has been touched. He is, then, when it comes to sound, a sort of Don Juan of songs. No song can satisfy him; or, better said, a song can only satisfy him once; it bores him the second time around. And because of this, the Don Juan of songs needs and demands a new song every day. He cannot live without this.

There is also, of course, that anguish over not listening to everything; that anxious desire for new songs and sounds; a very mortal musical Don Juan who says: one more and one more and another and another and another! One more song, please. One more new song!

Gluttony of the Ears

We can imagine another sin—the sin of gluttony of the eyes, sin of gluttony of the ears. A melomaniac incapable of saying: enough, I don't want to hear any more! A melomaniac who has tireless ears.

In this particular gluttony, there is an advantage for the insatiable: the stomach, despite all else, has physical limits, boundaries, concrete material, of the flesh and of the muscles, which at some point says—in its manner of speaking which is intense pain—it says, then: enough, I can't eat any more.

Well then, with the ears and the eyes, such a thing does not occur; the man who has been taken hold of by auditory gluttony possesses, in the anatomy of that famished auditory organ, a characteristic that aids him: there is no limit to the maximum load. This Don Juan of music keeps listening, listening, and listening, and doesn't stop, and wants to hear more and more and more, and his ears never hurt nor do they say: enough!

Auditory gluttony does not have, then, organic limits, with the exception of the intensity of the volume. We can damage our ears if we listen to music at high volume, but we cannot damage our ears if we listen to a lot of music (not even if it's music of low quality). It is not, therefore, a question of the quantity of sounds absorbed, as is the case with the stomach, which cannot bear more than a certain, though quite large, amount of comestible kilos. The sensibility of the auricular apparatus pertains only, then, to the volume of the sound. A man who rises early and straight away begins to eat will have to stop soon, even if using Roman methods of expelling the food and returning to the table.

The melomaniac, however, with his particular gluttony, can, quite early, at seven in the morning, start listening, and be finished only much later, well into the evening; and, during this time, he can listen to quite different sorts of songs, without stopping; and only go to bed after eighteen hours of uninterrupted listening. Therefore, the organism of a man-creature says this to the man-creature itself: there are limits to what you can eat, yet there are no limits to what you can hear or see.

Is this good? Is this bad?

And because of this, are the visual and auditory organs less animalistic, less organic—more human?

Orientation

1.
North, south, east, and west. An orchestra whose members change position according to the Sun. A symphony that lasts a day. It has the same duration as daylight. A symphony at the (tranquil) tempo of light.

2.
A sundial or a sort of sun clock: the hands of the clock—the musicians in the orchestra—slowly change position, to the rhythm of the light (rhythm of the light: a non-human rhythm).

3.
Orientation—disorientation. The conductor as true north on the compass: when you're lost, look to him.

4.
The disorientation of the musicians is spatial, not temporal. When they are lost, they are lost in the second, in the microsecond—as if these temporal units possessed square meters, detours, and crossroads.

5.

Time, then, has crossroads, and this is evident when one listens to an orchestra. At this precise moment, where does one go? And so a musician, in a manner that is imperceptible to the spectators, hesitates. But then looks at the conductor and perceives: *that is where I need to go.*

6.

As if the trajectory of fingers on the strings of a harp, for example, were truly a trajectory. And it really is: the minuscule march of fingers between the strings is a march, a change in position. A finger, between one string and the next, might get lost the way a child gets lost in the forest. Where was I going?—thinks the finger that (for someone looking at it) appears to levitate.

7.

The conductor as the one who best knows the route through time. He is an immobile traveler. He travels with the ear, not with the feet. He has walked this way many times, which is to say: he has listened a lot.

Peripeteia

Element of a tragedy. For Aristotle, "sudden change in conditions or destiny, which should occur in a verisimilar and necessary manner." Peripeteias in music ("the sudden change in destiny"), a quick description: that which seemed to be dying now grows and is stronger. That which was about to be elevated suddenly fell down.

The number of peripeteias that occur in a song, count them. And think about whether there is a minimum number or maximum limit—a median number of peripeteias, which surprise the listener sufficiently, but not too often. How many peripeteias does a song have, how many sudden changes in destiny? This is a relevant question.

Beethoven and his peripeteias. Mozart and his mischief.

A song without peripeteias: for falling asleep.

What is Music—Is There Music—with Letters?

Such is verbal music. Every letter is a sound, of course, and the relationship between letters makes that which is a sentence on the page into something that is a song for the person who reads.

A sentence by Clarice Lispector, for example. Which should be read aloud, not as someone who reads nor as someone who sings, but as someone who works the strings of an instrument that is different than all the instruments of an orchestra, a verbal-instrument.

No brass, no strings, no percussion, no anything: letters, letters!

"Watching the arrival of men and machines, the horses patiently pondered the position of their hooves."

A musical instrument that plays p (the letter p): *the horses patiently pondered the position of their hooves.*

Manner of Entrance

Doors that force the body to stoop or force the body to leap; to turn to the side or go up on tiptoes; extremely short doors that only allow the entrance of a crawling body. Doors with an entrance code, with a password that is only given to some—to family members, close friends. Doors that open with a light touch, others that require a forceful push, much strength, and muscle; revolving doors, which seem to turn the person entering them into a childish form of still seeming like a human. Doors of all sizes, shapes, and colors.

Does music have a door, a place through which one enters? One, two, many, none? Where does one enter?

Through the front door, the one that is on display for all to see. That is a type of music.

Where does one enter?

There is no door; you have to bring along tools for busting it open, for knocking it down. Another kind of music.

But yes, sometimes, being familiar with other, different cities helps the ear, and even helps the other elements of the spirit.

For example, walking through the Medina of Marrakesh and passing by the hundred thousand different doors. On the same street, passing by seven houses, there are seven different doors—tall ones, short ones, blue ones, purple ones, red ones, so on and so forth.

"How do I enter this song that I don't understand?" they ask a sensible melomaniac. And he replies:

"Go to Marrakesh and look (don't listen, just look)."

The Moment

Nicolau de Cusa spoke "of the coincidence of the maximum and the minimum in God."
Thus in certain songs.

The End of the Concert

The end of the concert, the strange sensation that the orchestra—which has long since abandoned the space and retreated into the wings—ultimately remains there, still playing in a fully empty space.

When does that which we have heard cease to sound, when do the ears close to the sound? As if there were, in truth, two different durations of a piece of music—one collective, public, and the other individual and private.

There is, obviously, an external duration of a piece of music—and the end of this is felt by all at the same moment (and thus the synchronized applause). If a public end to the sound did not exist, a concert would be constantly interrupted, by clapping hands or by people leaving (which is even what happens when things go poorly).

But, indeed, there is a second end to the music; an end, in this case, that is private, personal; an end, therefore, that is unsynchronized: after the concert, thirty minutes later, there is still someone whistling a tune they've heard; and there is also, mere seconds after the concert ends, someone who is already talking about something else—the weather, politics, or the next day's projects.

And there are even many other ways to leave a concert (or not to leave).

For example, there are those who, at the end, remain in the auditorium for a long time, sometimes seated, as if recuperating from a brief and fleeting illness; an illness that lasted an hour, but which weakened the body, and perhaps—who knows?—certain ancient convictions. And these people in recovery remain seated for a few long minutes, as if recalling the last sounds that lingered there after the orchestra took its leave. As if they were collectors of the nearly secret prominent moments, vibrations, echoes, which still tarry forth.

As in these lines of Tomas Tranströmer:
"The book that one drops while falling asleep
remains open,
as if wounded by gunshot, at the edge of the bed."

The Army

Let's think about the conductor and the elements of the orchestra.

Sometimes a human name is located behind the name of a musical instrument. A musician is reduced to a man who draws close to certain strings, brasses, or percussion instruments. Historical injustices, of course. It is Umberto Eco who speaks of the importance (but also the impossibility) of "citing the names of all the participants of the battle of Waterloo." So we cite one name: Napoleon, and we multiply that name a hundred times, a thousand times, or more. But it's not enough.

Monument to the unknown soldier. Monument to the musician whose name we shall never know.

Magician's Biography

One of the most famous magicians, Robert-Houdin (not to be confused with Houdini), was a watchmaker in his youth.

We ask—how does one make something that capable of astonishing us? Exactly like this: knowing how things function in the back; having a map of the wings of the stage, a clear map of the backside of the world. A clear map of the dark part.

But not always is the hidden part of what we see made up of gear wheels that advance in each other's grooves. Sometimes, the backside of the visible world is unexpected, or even chaotic.

So—thus it is, then, that a wise man who teaches music is facing some young musicians who immediately, first thing in the morning, want to make something ostentatiously new. The new! The new! The astonishing! Thus the ambition of the young musician.

But the sensible pedagogue advises them to remain calm and says:

"Like Robert-Houdin, the magician: please, first learn the watchmaker's art."

The advice is received with shock, but the pedagogue *lightly* explains (it's important not to explain everything, to explain only lightly; a light, brief explanation; an explanation that leaves space for the curiosity of those who hear it. And explanation that diminishes ignorance, yet does not annul dissatisfaction):

"It's not about knowing how the material elements function," says the pedagogue, "it's know about knowing how the mechanical wheels function, it's about knowing how time functions, which is quite different."

The novice musician, who up to that point had only brought the watch to her ear to hear the minimal sound of the hands, is now interested in the rest of it—in what is hidden, in the essential.

But once more, young musician: don't learn everything, don't perceive everything; save some dissatisfaction in your fingers and your head so that your desire to compose is maintained and grows.

The Watchmaker, the Musician

Let's continue our pondering of this biographical fact—the magician Robert-Houdin was a watchmaker in his youth.

In truth, the watchmaker is an investigator of the immaterial. He pretends to have manual ability to fix and adjust mechanisms, but at heart what he does is think about the world and about human finitude. He fixes and adjusts watches, but this is, in a certain way, the first part of a philosophy course. He is there because someone advised him to read the philosophers and be patient; he learns the art of the watchmaker because he knows that despair is only alleviated through a specific discipline. Contained discipline and despair, this is a mixture that, when properly channeled, can turn out quite well.

And yes, that young man, that young woman, now that they know how to think and now that they have dominated, in swift fashion, the difficult manual art of the watchmaker, sit down at the piano to compose. They did not get ahead of themselves, therefore.

Because it is necessary to start at the beginning, or even before the beginning. Never start in the middle, and never, ever, try to start at the end. These are basic recommendations.

Your Excellency wishes to compose music? Well, first start by perceiving something about time, about rhythm.

This is what I propose to you: a two-year watchmaker's course. Are you prepared? Do you really want to be a musician? Well then, come forward!

(It is said that Robert-Houdin admired pianists and, in particular, the capacity they had to read music and play at the same time. In his diary, he recounted a juggling exercise he performed: "I would place a book in front of me and, while my four balls were whirling in the air, I grew accustomed to reading without faltering." He would read and not drop a thing.

Learning, then, to be a musician via strange paths.)

Definition

Harmony? Good and Evil meet each other halfway down the path and become indistinct from one another; a hundred things become one; it is imperceptible who is receiving and who is giving.

Pythagoreans say that "Music is the harmony of contraries, the unification of the many and the agreement of the disagreeable."

It's a beautiful definition.

Luxury

And if a man were to look at the notes of a piece of music as if some of them were a luxury good?

"And Socrates, upon seeing luxury objects put out for sale, exclaimed: 'There are so many things I do not need!'" (Schopenhauer)

Eliminating the luxurious in a piece of music; to retain only the necessary and indispensable goods (the necessary notes). That which the ear—and the rest of the organism—need to remain alive in a sensible way.

Sometimes, an entire piece of music—from the first note to the last—is, because of its homogeneous inefficacy, a true luxury object.

Walking through the city, hearing here and there, on one radio station and another: *so much unnecessary interruption of silence.*

Obsessive Melomaniac

Failed attempts to define an obsessive melomaniac:
The body as an enlargement of the ear.
The body as an appendage of the ear.
Man as that which is located in between the ears.
Man: that which exists in order to listen.
Man: animal made for listening.
He is distinguished from other animals because he knows how to distinguish different notes.
(And take note, indeed: what other animals separate Do from Re?)
But of course listening does not end with the ear. It begins there.

The Third Sound

And take note, indeed: what other animals separate Do from Re?

The fact is that animals have, to simplify it here, two sounds in the world: the sound that announces pleasure and the sound that announces pain. And perhaps a third sound: that which announces nothing relevant.

And perhaps this third sound is the sound that announces boredom.

"Hear that? That is the sound that announces nothing, or that announces nothingness. What of it?"

However, it is said: announcing nothing and announcing nothingness are two quite different sonorous announcements. Announcing nothing is an informational failure: I come with nothing either out of forgetfulness or incompetence.

It is another thing altogether to *announce nothingness*. Announcing nothingness is on the order of the most frightful omens. Tomorrow, nothingness. Day after tomorrow, nothingness. That's what is coming.

This is on the same level—or perhaps even worse—in terms of instilling terror, as the announcement of a devastating storm headed this way.

Worse, then, than a bad storm is the coming of nothingness, which is neither bad nor good—on the contrary, as the distant cynic would say.

Because, in fact, when it comes to a concrete enemy, you can resist, argue, create obstacles.

But nothingness . . . how does it draw near? At what speed does this announced nothingness approach? Is it coming fast or slow? Is it coming from above or below? From nowhere at all, you'll reply, and at no speed whatsoever, you'll say. Yet, indeed, that is exactly what frightens us. How does something that doesn't approach, doesn't shift position, approach us?

My dear, don't fight it—what is coming, what is arriving, is nothingness. And against it, against nothingness—that non-fighter par excellence—all fighting fails.

That music announce evil or good, violence or melancholy, pleasure or pain that hurts bad in the wrong spot, that it announce everything and each thing in particular, but that it never announce nothingness—this is what is asked of music.

Concert Hall

Thinking of the concert hall as an enormous enumerated alphabet.

The seats go from A to Z, this illustrates the simple alphabet. What is changed, then, is that there are many As and Bs: B5, B6, B7, etc.

It's clear that we don't encounter different ways of drawing the same letter, however that would be a good experiment. The B of B7 cannot be the same as the B of B8. Imagining, then, a letter drawn in a different manner; imagining a completely different seat (seat B7 is soft, seat B8 is hard as all get out!). In sum, imagining a hall in which every seat is unique.

When we're speaking of assigned seats, of private seats, of year-long subscriptions which mean that a certain person always sits in the same place for months on end, this sort of individualization of place, let's say, should be taken to its ultimate consequences. Different seats (according to people's particular tastes) and even the possibility that this seat (or the back of the seat in front of it) might also come with photographs of the family, meaningful phrases for that specific person, etc. Make yourself at home, this spot is yours.

On the Concertgoer

Sonorous occupation of the face (of the person listening): your face was occupied by the sounds you heard.

Conductor

An irresponsible man walks toward the front of the orchestra. Lacking arms, he conducts the sounds up and down by furrowing his brow, opening and closing his eyes, a sudden smirk at the corner of his mouth. The orchestra follows this conductor the way one follows an individual master. We are dealing with an orchestra with ever-attentive eyes, an orchestra of details, an orchestra that sees, not large movements of the body, but that which is slower and more subtle in the face.

Late Afternoon, Sun

Music evaporates from the surfaces that were placed at a certain angle under a certain light from the Sun. At six in the afternoon, summertime, Lisbon.

Not Breaking Things

A man is walking and, under his feet, something happens; there is a mole-orchestra; an orchestra beneath the earth that is playing so out of tune that it makes the ground shake. This is what is commonly called an earthquake, the earth shakes because a wrong note was played.

Sometimes all it takes is one wrong note: a Mi that shouldn't have appeared at that moment—and then everything collapses, like something that is always at the very edge. And, indeed, that is what happens: the earth and all the sounds of the world are always at the edge; and when that buried orchestra, that orchestra comprised of our dead, that orchestra that plays in our memories, in the heavens and on earth, when it produces a false note, this is what occurs: the earth shakes! Two centimeters, maybe three, to one side, to the other—but yes: the earth shakes because one of the strings was out of tune.

And being out of tune is this: it is losing the center; it is accelerating or stopping abruptly, it's not respecting the placid velocity of things (things—even things at rest—have a velocity in their manner of being still; a velocity in the manner in which they await a human hand in action).

A cup has a restful velocity, an anxiety and also an invitation to the hand that surrounds it and hasn't yet grabbed hold of it. All things, all objects, tools that man has placed upon the table, are elements that demand a serene sound to surround them, a sound that does not go out of tune. And this, then, is the absolute out-of-tuneness of the things of the world: a cup that falls to the ground and clamorously breaks! There, at the middle of this clamor, this is the material definition of being out of tune. The breaking of things is the final out-of-tuneness of things. And yes: an orchestra that is in tune is what keeps the material elements of the world undisturbed and defended. Music is not made exclusively for man; objects also absorb it. It is necessary so that things don't fall down.

Witnessing

Is the listener not a witness? If there are ocular-witnesses, aren't there also auditory-witnesses?

Imagine that all the events of the world should have visual-witnesses, auditory-witnesses, gustatory-witnesses, olfactory-witnesses, and tactile-witnesses.

An auto accident, for example: there should be a visual witness, but also witnesses who are attentive to every detail of the different senses. And imagining, thus, a melomaniac-witness, a witness with a well above average auditory aptitude.

Imagine, then, an auditory witness of a scream and a witness of the sounds of the quotidian world, banal sounds. A melomaniac who follows contemporary music will be capable, we believe, of detecting every sound of the world and elevating it to the central element of his narrative. For example, with the auto accident: the screeching of the tires, its rhythm, its intensity, the duration of the sound of the tires screeching, that which an auditory witness who isn't a good listener would classify as "a loud screeching," the attentive contemporary melomaniac would be able, from this same sound, to create a detailed description. He would, thus, transform the shapeless sonorous description into a sonorous description with a shape—or rather, with length, height, and width.

At heart, it is this: we are almost always visual witnesses of the world, and rarely are our other organs which are capable of witnessing called into action. Therefore, training the ear. That's a start.

On Dance

Children dance as a way to calm down. They are lost, and their mother said, explicitly, before they left home: When you're lost, dance, so that you'll get tired.

It's necessary to have energy in order to be afraid, and dance is a musical form of getting tired, of losing the energy necessary for fear. It seems to me like an option, like any other.

Where to Start; Time

Imitating a painting, which has neither beginning nor end, has no narrative—the eyes don't start at the top on the left side, nor do they advance along an undisturbed, leisurely, straight line, in some stable, organized fashion. Looking at a painting is something else; it's a sudden leap, a form of suddenly falling into a trap that combines color and shape. We start seeing at the brushstroke, at the point that most seduces the eye, not the point that says: Beginning. (And there is no point that says "beginning.") Thus the image becomes an unbegun, unfinished thing in the world, a thing that is just there and will remain there. Imagine music in this way: as a brushstroke, as something into which you cannot enter at any point. Not having a beginning or middle or end of music; music is there and remains there, and you are the one who enters and exits when your body requires it or can no longer bear it. What determines the beginning of a piece of music isn't the music itself: rather, it is the decision of the person who listens to it. I am beginning to listen now and, therefore, the music is starting. I have now finished listening and, therefore, the music has come to an end. The music itself is a sonorous brushstroke, a rhythmic form of occupying auditory space, space that isn't measured in the same way as the space of material bodies. But there is an auditory space—a site, an area, a square, a rectangle, into which sounds enter. And if you call that rectangle or square "time," you aren't far off, but you're off. It isn't exactly in the space of time that music exists and forges ahead—time can neither be seen nor heard, nor can it be touched. Time is, therefore, a mute and invisible thing, without scent or taste, it is a nothingness lacking volume and shape, the nothingness that crushes and dominates us.

Friendship

Elie Wiesel in *Testament of a Murdered Jewish Poet*: "he was my friend because he allowed me to take action." Thus, too, with certain songs. You listen, but with free hands; you can do things while you listen; you can take action, I'll follow you (not at your side, but underneath you, and keep you from falling). Like a table. Table: machine that keeps things from falling; having someone at our side who keeps us from falling, that's the important thing. A sort of human table, a spiritual machine-table (combination of three elements of the world—object, machine, and spirit). Songs that keep us from falling: the essential ones.

In sum—songs that allow us to take action: song-friends. Songs that impede our actions: enemies in song form.

Aerial Occupation of Space

Aerial occupation of space, that is music. As if the owner wanted something that is above ground, yet not exactly the ground; it doesn't take up square meters. An aerial estate, long songs: a different manner of occupying space: an invisible shape with no fixed point. Taking up space from above.

Music cannot be located on the axes of ordinates and abscissas; we can imagine a melody as a precise graph of the successive positions of the notes, but an (invisible) graph that is taking flight, carried by a strong wind, erratic in its movements and not localizable (but not like a piece of paper blown by the wind, nothing like that).

Sounds are not situated in space, this is the central issue. A note that is heard is not located at 4x 15y; rather, it is something that occupies, at most, a position in time, as if time were also a thing with a surface—but no, but no; unfortunately not.

Atoms, Particles

And indeed: that chemical process of drawing particles and atoms near each other, and through this chemical approximation bringing visible and practical substances into the world. Seeing music and its notes as chemical elements. In short, might there be something similar to H2O in music? Does Re-Re-Fa create a sonorous substance? A new chemical element in the air that produces a sensation in the ear (like a strong, cold wind)?

It's necessary to pay attention to aerial encounters and collisions; the way two sounds fight or procreate high in the air above the ground. Because we are dealing with an ancient manner of sending flying elements into the air. Much earlier than the airplane, therefore.

Average and Central Music

Every language has a certain sonorousness, and each country's anthem should ultimately be this (not some song, as if chosen at random out of all the different possible sounds), it should, indeed, be the precise average of the fundamental sounds of a language, of the nasal or throaty or sibilant or high or low sounds or AAAs and EEEEs and OOOOs and usss, fffs, etc.

This, then, should be possible: recite all of the words of a given language, all of the words in the dictionary, say them out loud, one by one, and record them. And from this, afterwards, through some complex, yet precise, system—the way seven plus seven is fourteen—from this recording of all the words of a given language (words from the first to last pages of the dictionary) there should result a song, an unmistakable song, a succession of sounds that would be nothing more than the precise average of all the sounds.

The question is: can we calculate this average? Can we make statistical elements underlie a language?

At bottom, conflicts, wars, and great battles are always about imposing certain sounds (and also gestures). You win when you sing your song, you lose when your enemy sings his song in your home (which is, ultimately, no longer your home, because your song no longer tarries within).

Statistics, anthem, sound, war.

And then the home, the fire, which does not destroy, but warms.

Joy, Sadness

There is a limit how much sadness in music we can bear—this limit is determined by us, by our capacity. With regard to contentment, it's different.

The joy of an individual, when it surpasses a certain limit, becomes unbearable (and dangerous) for others.

"Sad tune, borne only
by those who have not lost their joy."
Adélia Prado

Who can bear a joyful tune? Those who know that there is certainly a much different song coming after this one.

Domestic Sound

Can a domestic sound be a short love song?
This poem, also by Adélia Prado ("Teaching"):
"My mother thought study
the finest thing in the world.
It isn't.
The finest thing in the world is feeling.
That day, at night, with my father working late,
she said to me:
'Poor thing, doing hard labor at this time of night.'
She set out bread and coffee, left a pot of hot water on the stove.
She spoke not of love.
That luxurious word."
Can a domestic sound be a short love song?
Response: pot of hot water on the stove.

Head Facing Out

If you turned your ear inward, what would you hear? Your thoughts? The mechanical noise of the organs that remain alive? And what would you see (with eyes facing in, not out)? Any minor film, any rudimentary music by a novice cellist is better than this.

Why, then, are our ears, eyes, nose, etc. facing out? Because out there the spectacle, despite all else, has more variety.

Musical Modalities

Songs of aerobic resistance, marathoner songs. And songs of the hundred-meter sprinter (they arrive quickly, then are tired).

It is necessary to create an athletic taxonomy of songs. High jump-songs, long jump-songs, weightlifting-songs, shot put-songs. For example, a song that lifts a weight from down low to on high, that lifts the weight of the listener towards the sky, is completely different from another song (shot put) that tosses our weight off into the distance—this song, which obliges us (after it ends) to go gather the core of us from up ahead (we have become light because our weight was thrown far off in front of us). And indeed, this is just one example—there are infinite athletic variations of music. Music with hurdles, music without hurdles. Etc., etc.

The Remainder and the Shadow

1.
What we see is always a remainder, what is left over from the invisible (from what you have never seen and never will see).
"Roots are clearly never seen
but you know
that they support the tree.
To be just,
think of the roots."
Giánnis Ritsos
We sometimes feel this in a song. We hear the music-tree. But to be just, we would have to dig.

2.
And we should even think about the shadow of a sound, about the temporary black vestige that the note leaves on the ground, as if it were a terrestrial phantom—the lower part of the sound, the part you can see (but not hear).
But the sound will not create shadows in the way we understand them. The sound's shadow will not depend on light (or perhaps it will, perhaps it will).
Light hits the sound, and from this invisible, mute collision, a sensation will result—listening to a song in the sun is not the same as listening to it in a closed compartment.
What you feel when you listen to a song is perhaps, in the end, the song's shadow.

Sensibility and Function

The praise of musicians and their almost extra-human, super-human sensibility, pre-human and beyond-human sensibility. Well then, this is what is being referred to in relation to the pre-human, the perception of the movements of the earth and the sea, for example, which animals can sense well before any visual or auditory sign becomes relevant for human eyes and ears. Descriptions of elephants that flee from the ocean, running, a day before a tsunami invades the coastline.

Therefore, some musicians could be hired to play near the sea; tsunami-detecting orchestras.

Placed at well-chosen locations at various points along the coast, there are the earthquake-and tsunami-detecting orchestras! When the musicians start to flee from the ocean; when the musicians interrupt their rehearsals and start shouting warnings that an earthquake is going to take place soon, we should follow them, without hesitation.

Thereby putting the sensibility of musicians at the service of terrestrial disasters and catastrophes.

Instead of lifeguards, post musicians next to the maritime surface; saving lives by anticipation. The musician detects the danger in advance, and then afterwards we can call the lifeguard. The musician doesn't swim, but points; isn't a scientist, but signals a coming storm or disturbance in the sea before they are manifest; warns of a big wave coming while the small wave is still right there, looking like it's there to stay. Thus, then, in this fictional country, these duos near the sea—a musician and a scientist; a musician and a lifeguard.

Auditory Shoulders

An orchestra that plays upon our shoulders. Like someone who suddenly feels a burning sensation in the nape of their neck; the symptom of some sort of spasm and, ultimately . . . it was an orchestra. Having a weight on your shoulders versus having a song on your shoulders. Shouldering a burden versus having a melody shoulder you.

Losing your Hearing

What would you miss the most, having lost your hearing? The information you would have been given via the human voice?

To this response, after much thought, we would probably reply: the greatest loss would be music. Because sonorous information can be replaced by various other types of information—written information, etc. However, music cannot be transmitted through other means. It is not information. If you become deaf, you will lose music.

Brief Notes on Bloom-Literature

Technical-Literary Dictionary
Manifesto
of the Bloom Books

One of the many (definitive) ways
to make literature

Prefatory Note

There are infinite (definitive) ways to make literature. This is a manifesto of Bloom-Literature. We can be definitive in one direction at one time and, then, the next time, be completely, enthusiastically definitive, but in the other direction.

Two Bloom-books:
The Left Leg of Paris Followed by Roland Barthes and Robert Musil
and
Voyage to India

Though *Voyage to India* is many hybrids and, perhaps, in this case, it is also a Bloom-Literature hybrid with some other thing, and *The Left Leg...* is also perhaps not definitively Bloom-Literature. In fact, perhaps not even this dictionary is pure-Bloom. And that seems fine to me.

Abstract—All literature is abstract; stones are concrete. Not to accept this is to accept literature as a copier of the concrete, like a second table or a second house.

The word house (let's imagine that the house belongs to Ms. Gertrude), the word house isn't a second house for Ms. Gertrude. Ms. Gertrude—poor thing—only has one house: let's not deceive her, then, with the illusion of a second abode. The house—in this or any other sentence—is an abstracted house, or rather: a literary house.

Literature is not a copy of the objects in the world: the house is not a house, and the table is not a table. Literature has its own objects, completely distinct from those that exist in the life of the living.

Don't mistake a writer for an arranger of furniture.

Accumulate—You should not accumulate information or narrative episodes. Perplexities are what should be accumulated.

Literature requires specialists of mysteries. But not the mystery of detective stories with a determined end: the murderer is discovered. We are dealing (in literature) with a specialist who studies mystery, increasing it. To study mystery is to increase it, not diminish it. In a certain manner, Bloom-literary criticism is also this: not diminishing perplexities, but increasing them.

At the end of a Bloom text, or even at the end of a Bloom sentence, the reader should not-know more facts than she not-knew before. This, however, is not a method of increasing ignorance, but a method for increasing curiosity.

To accumulate is, then, to diminish, to make more scarce.

Advance—There are two types of men, just as there are two types of sentences: those that run as fast as their legs run and those that run as fast as their head runs.

In the sentence, the head is the part of the sentence that imagines.

Advice—Paternalistic sentences should be left to parents and eliminated from (Bloom) literature.

Aristocracy—Every sentence with words that aren't understood by the masses should be banned. Words that are individually obscure are obscure when they could be clear.

However, every sentence understood by the masses should be banned. Sentences that are individually clear and obvious are imbecilic.

I perceive all the words clearly, but the text, not entirely—such is the effect of Bloom-literature.

Sentences are elevated by the threat of their strangeness. Words debase themselves with the strangeness they exhibit.

Every word that individually requires investigation should be eliminated.

Every sentence that does not require investigation should also be eliminated.

B

Bloom—A universally applicable name for any thing or occurrence. Bloom-chair, Bloom-book, Bloom-death, Bloom-relationship.

Book—A book should be a bound peril.

C

Canine—There are canine sentences. Ready to obey their master, their reader.

Being at the reader's disposal: canine-sentence.

Substituting canine-sentences for wolf-sentences and tiger-sentences. The reader who experiments with putting her head there.

Verses that frighten the reader. But also, at the same time, verses that make the reader take precautions. Faced with danger, some flee (method of precaution 1), while others investigate strategies for drawing closer (method of precaution 2). These are the good readers. The others: good cowards.

Character—Is an organic thing that should emerge and disappear in a single sentence. In 100 consecutive sentences, there can be 100 characters.

In a Bloom-book, characters are secondary and sentences are primary. The presence of people is merely a pretext so that language may speak.

What does it matter who does what?

The organisms that exist in texts push ideas forward. An organism without ideas is just an organism.

Cruelty—We can also talk about the necessity of a medium level of cruelty in a literary sentence. A pious sentence possesses less literature than a cruel sentence. If you doubt this, pick up a text and start keeping count.

D

Darkness—In Bloom-literature, darkness is not the invisible, but rather the evident. The explicit is merely a mistake made by the gaze, which should have detected the mystery instead. Bloom-literature restores this gaze. I don't want to see in order to understand, I want to see in order not to understand. You do not discover evidence, you discover mystery. Every object in your daily life is an insult to your capacity to become dark. Replace: *can you please clarify that?* with: *can you please obscure that?*

Only transform the impossible into something clear and evident.

Diagram—If a book is reducible to a diagram, it is because the diagram can be enlarged enough to give origin to a book. Everything that is reducible is the size of the reduction. If a text is reducible to a diagram, why present the text?

Bloom-literature is not reducible.

A diagram that synthesizes a text is proof that the text is useless.

Every sentence should be a diagram: the essence of both an explosion and an implosion.

A diagram is a substance of highest energies and the median energy of a Bloom-sentence should possess the energy of a diagram.

A Bloom-literature text is not the sum total of the energy of each of its sentences. It is not: Energy of sentence 1 + energy of sentence 2 + energy of sentence 3, and so on and so forth. No. It's the inverse, that is: it is half the inverse. Or rather: the energy of sentence 1 is the same quantity as the whole text, and the same quantity as that which exists in every one of the sentences that follow it.

And energy is not something that can be abridged.

A Bloom-sentence will have more energy than an entire non-Bloom text.

It isn't one step at a time: in one leap, one can advance to the seventh floor.

A seventh floor that is reached in a single movement is higher than a seventh floor that is reached step by step. You might think that the inverse is true, given the effort required, but no. All time that is lost is time that is lost.

Dictionary (see "muscles")—All Bloom-literature is created in opposition to dictionaries. It is the battle between fixed point and a shove (non-fixation). All that is fixed is useless; all that is *only this way* is useless. What interests Bloom-literature is everything that *is this way* but could even *be this other way*. But, if we think it through, there is nothing that is not interesting to Bloom-literature, because there is nothing that cannot be the other way. All that is is a hypothesis of being.

Every word can always signify something else. Each word has thousands of hypothetical existences. The common dictionary defines the most common hypothetical existence, the median-hypothesis. Bloom-literature knows well the process of calculating the median, because what it tries to get out of every word is its marginal hypotheses, its extreme, rare values.

Money does not have a spinal column: it folds for all fingers.

Dilution—Texts that dilute an idea for thirty pages, transforming ideas into usurious objects, are falsifications. The method of dilution is a method of non-Bloom literature, of an impoverished literature that stays at home for six months parceling out the only piece of bread it has in order to survive for six months. But there is always the possibility of leaving the house to find victuals. Who would have thought it?

Of course there is a difference between diluting over 100 pages of text and diluting within a single sentence. Diluting two sentences could be a Bloom-method in the event that they are followed by other, different chemical processes. A concentration at great velocity, after two diluted sentences, could have a greater concentration of Bloom than that same concentration coming after a sentence with a normal distribution of substances.

The Bloom-method has as its foundation the constant alteration of processes; but dilution being a break from this change is not the same as change being a break from dilution.

One should not mistake a trace for something that is diluted. A dilution does not result in a trace, but in a weak concentration. A trace is not a weak concentration of a substance. A trace is something powerful that becomes visible and points to or pushes toward many other powerful substances. A trace is an incredibly strong concentration of ideas, images, sounds, etc. Or rather: it is the inverse of something that is diluted.

It is more difficult to dilute the trace of a thing than to dilute the thing itself. It's obvious: if you spill water on a text, you'll ruin the text.

E

Energy—It isn't the letters; the energy of a text is invisible and of utmost importance. The energy of a text could be quantified by the consequences it provokes in readers. How many lines of verse originated from a given line of verse? How many films, how many paintings, how many sentences, how many actions?

The energy of a text is the future of that text. What will occur in the world because of its existence.

Equilibrium—Scales and business deals are things that should be equilibrated. Literature is not a business deal between the writer and the reader. It is a threat, a devastation, a theft, an unequilibrated action that demands the existence of a future that reorganizes things and names.

Names of disproportionate weight. As if a single sentence could have a tendency to rise toward the sky and descend below the earth.

F

Foreigner—A foreign sentence isn't a sentence in a language that is not our own. It is, however, a sentence that we don't immediately recognize; that we can neither recognize nor explain immediately. In Bloom-literature, all sentences should be foreign.

G

Genetics—It is evident that every word has its own genes: it comes from a place and displays its markers. However, what matters are not so much the individual genes of each word, but rather the way that the various genes of the various words are combined. A writer is someone who conjoins genes, promotes intermixture and fecundation. And every uncommon admixture of two words produces a new genetic combination.

The number of genes is limited; the combination of genes, unlimited. A writer of clichés is convinced there are only 656 possible combinations of genes. It is another sort of morality, this combinatory chastity between words.

Geography—Geographical localization is a literary error. Each character operates in places, and that's enough. Names of cities, names of countries, of neighborhoods, of houses, of people, all localized names are unnecessary. The literary text is not lost, but it also isn't localized.

Where can you find this sentence? What is the location of this sentence?

Where? This is not a question for literature to answer.

What do we do while we're alive? This is a question for literature to pose.

Characters with countries and geographically fixed events are heavy characters and events.

That which is light can be transported with us, that which is heavy is abandoned in its place (no one takes it with them).

Either an action occurs in multiple geographies, or an action occurs in a place that doesn't have a name on the map: literature.

Where did this take place?

It took place in literature.

The only geography within literature is the sentence, the word.

Geometry—Every sentence with geometry has too much geometry.

Literature should function like a swarm of bees, and disorder has never allowed for a measuring tape.

All measurements taken of a thing are acts of violence upon that thing.

Measuring is imprisonment by number.

All Bloom-literature is immeasurable. There is no correspondence between four words and the number four.

Instruments of measurement for solid substances come up against liquid literature, instruments of measurement for liquid substances come up against solid or gaseous literature.

Every literary solid will behave as a liquid.

Every literary liquid will behave as a solid.

The death of literature begins at the moment when the reader is able to anticipate the behavior of sentences to come.

The only law of sentences is to have a different law.

H

Hemorrhage—All clear prose should instate a tendency toward hemorrhage. As if the sentence always already existed on the verge of bleeding, of rupturing: of one part of the sentence renouncing the meaning of the other part.

All hemorrhages are the effect of a separation. All separations are the promise of two beginnings at a distance from each other, of two recommencements. If half the sentence separates itself from the other half, we obtain two texts that are each moving toward their own sides, like two animals. And every animals wants its own food, its private place for digestion, its shameful defecation.

A text that bleeds is an indication of a multiplication of meanings.

Prose that avoids hemorrhages at all costs is infantile prose.

Hermaphrodite—The true Bloom-sentence doesn't contain a person with a sex, it contains a person with sexes.

Motors that move in two directions are more promising than motors that move in just one.

The letters in themselves—the alphabet—have no inclination. Only in words do the feminine and masculine exist. However, the sentence can reconstitute the powerful neutrality that exists in the alphabet. If Mrs. Bloom is female at the beginning of the sentence, she can end up, at the end of the sentence, masculine, with a deep voice and body hair. Let's not complicate things: in literature, the characteristics of the characters depend solely on the letters that the writer puts in the sentences. She is a female character only because *she* is written: it begins with an s. If it began with an h, instead of an s, that same character would be: *he*, a male character. Why, then, place so much importance on the placement of an s or an h?

Hesitations—The writer should not hesitate, but sentences should. And the reader should too.

The certainty of the one creating should instill doubt in the one observing.

Every spectator will become perturbed in the face of an imperturbable action.

Every intelligent sentence is a sentence that hesitates between zero and one.

Every unequivocal decision should give rise to thousands of different decisions.

Only great certainty will provoke disturbance.

Literature should be a certainty that causes disturbance and not a disturbance whose effect is certainty.Literature brings forth an unsynchronized kingdom.

Hybrid—There is no action that can turn a text into a hybrid. A text is naturally hybrid. Language spontaneously intermixes.

There is only a way to impede hybridism in language. Purity in language is artificial.

I

Individuality—Every sentence is individual. And every text is individual. The difficulty in making sure that every sentence is individual—1—and that every text, in its entirety, is also individual—1—is the difficulty of the writer.

Any given book does not need any other book.

Any given sentence does not need any other sentence.

And if sentences are collective, they are not individual. If they are not individual—one—then they don't exist: they can be eliminated.

Every sentence that needs others in order to be strong should be eliminated.

Apply the brutality of immediate selection to every sentence. Every sentence either speaks or remains silent. Every sentence has its own moment to prove whether it is worth being in existence. Every sentence has fifteen seconds of existence for the reader. In these fifteen seconds, it will have to prove that it deserves to exist in the next fifteen seconds.

Not being individual is not to exist.

Intensity—The intensity of a sentence demonstrates the manners of the sentence. A sentence that isn't very intense is a poorly mannered sentence for the reader. Why? Because you shouldn't waste someone's time.

Interference—In any text, one sentence should interfere with another. To interfere is to enter into a space that doesn't belong to you. A sentence should enter into the previous sentence and the following sentence. But we aren't talking about continuity and harmony among the sentences here. On the contrary: a sentence should enter the ones that surround it like a hand drill at work: as something that produces misshapen disturbances and noises.

A sentence should disturb the understanding of the previous sentence. When we judge a sentence to be calm, that's when another comes along and infiltrates it.

Certain interferences can be subtle, but some should function like explosions. The shrapnel from one sentence enters into the next sentence and this process produces wounds. Or rather: situations to be resolved.

But pay attention: shrapnel doesn't produce scars, shrapnel produces wounds, and the wounds, over time, can produce scars.

Shrapnel that directly produces scars is a falsification.

Only dead sentences do not interfere.

Inundation—A text can suddenly be inundated. This is not a slow accumulation: inundation is a process of rapid conquest of space. It is a force that arises and quickly occupies space, taking the place of a previously dominant force. At the end of ten pages a certain tone in a sentence and a certain subject matter are suddenly swallowed up by a sentence with different contours. It's clear that one could construct a text made up of successive inundations. There is no recommended average amount of inundations per page. One inundation per sentence could be too much, or not.

Invention—Inventing is an ancient process, a process that is repeated. To invent is to imitate the process of inventing.

An invention is a non-superfluous imitation. An imitation is a redundant invention.

L

Legislation—Every sentence will be half legislation—imposition—and the other half an invitation, a request.

It is indispensable that every sentence give orders. And it is indispensable that the following sentences give orders that are symmetrical to the previous ones.

Poetry as legislation of contradictions: Make a sentence, and its opposite, into law—that is, make it obligatory.

These two symmetrical, contradictory, and irreconcilable laws are obligatory from this moment on. Thus, two lines of verse. And if the line is dense and absolute, this is what that single line is: two irreconcilable laws made obligatory.

M

Manners—Literature shouldn't have good manners. But it also shouldn't have bad manners—which is a different way of giving good manners a central position. Literature should be something beyond the extra-literary good and bad.

Map—Of course a sentence can produce a map. But if it does, the legend shouldn't be clear.

In literature, maps arise as clues. The first glance doesn't locate them. Nor does the second.

The map of clues and not of evidence is a method of prolonging the gaze. Imbeciles give a quick glance at a thing and say: There is nothing here to be pondered. The wise give a good long look.

In literature, the effective map isn't one that immediately shows us where we are, the destination, the paths. The efficient map in literature isn't one that has us walk the shortest distance to our destination, but precisely the inverse: one that makes us walk more.

What do you do with the map that a poem has given you? What do you do with the map that a novel has given you? The quantity and quality of things that you do demonstrates the effect of literature. Strong literature takes you someplace far away—and none of the paths leading from there are short.

And of course there are works of literature on different scales. Clarice Lispector wrote 100 pages about a cockroach. Thomas Mann wrote *Buddenbrooks*, the story of a family over the course of many generations.

However, the territory occupied by a work of literature doesn't depend on the territory occupied by the narrative. Or rather: the literary territory is not the 100 or 600 pages; it isn't the subject matter about the quotidian or about emperors. The territory of a work of literature is the space toward which that work pushes. A strong three-word line of poetry possesses more territory than six volumes of a boring monograph.

Maria—The name of all Bloom female characters. If there is more than one female character, they should be named Maria 2, Maria 3, etc.

If a Bloom writer, at the end of seven novels, introduces the 37th female character, she should designate her as: Maria (37).

The same logic should be maintained for male characters, this time using the name John as the basis. John 1, John 2, etc.

Bloom is a nickname. Not just for people, but also for the world.

Matter—The matter utilized is not words and letters, but rather intensity.

Only the present is intense.

Anticipation does not come before what is intense, but rather is the intensity before an event that may or may not also be intense.

We can suspend anticipation even within anticipation: and thus anticipation will not be sated, but will possess intensity. Bloom-moments do not need a moment that follows them.

Menu (see "urgency")—The choice of where to enter a text should come from the reader, not the writer. If a text only has one entryway, why enter? Entering through the same door as everyone else does not sit well with the Bloom-reader.

A Bloom-text may be read starting from page 60, 342, or 18. A Bloom-text may even be read starting from page 1.

Every sentence is a possible beginning to the text.

If a sentence has individual value, that sentence could be placed anywhere and could be read in any given order. Sentences whose individual value is dependent on the 65,743 previous sentences are sentences that do not have individual value.

A sentence is like an organism: it exists in the world alongside others; but it exists alone and will die alone.

There is, then, selfishness in the Bloom-sentence. Every sentence has an ego. It doesn't accept depending on others, it doesn't accept being less interesting than the others. No sentence sacrifices itself so that the following sentence shines.

Violating language with non-Bloom violence is to weaken certain sentences so that the effect of following sentences may become more intense.

Every sentence should act within the text as if the reader were going to die a second later. Say what you have to say quickly: this is what the Bloom-writer asks of every sentence.

Every sentence thus has a certain quality of urgency. As if someone were about to die and still anxiously wanted to hear these words.

If a sentence were a weakling, and the following one a weakling as well, and all this because up ahead a sentence is coming that allows for comprehension and thus produces a great intensity at long last—if sentences were like this, incredibly humble, then the reader would have already died and the intensity of the language would not yet have arrived.

To repeat: the Bloom-writer writes each sentence as if it were the last that the reader will read. The reader will die at the end of this sentence: this is the way the writer should think.

Morality—Morality is a force that impedes a sentence from saying what it has to say. Morality is the enemy of astonishing language, the enemy of language.

A moral sentence is not a sentence, it is a moral. An immoral sentence is an immorality, but it is also a sentence. It can be intense or not, that is different matter.

No one should hope for the kindness of a line of verse or a substance. Words are not kindhearted because they don't even have a heart.

One should not confuse the anatomy of the alphabet with human anatomy. An error of the moralistic texts.

N

Negotiations—A sentence does not negotiate with readers, nor does the writer negotiate with sentences.

The sentence imposes itself on the Bloom-writer, who imposes it on the Bloom-reader.

Certain writers impose sentences on the language. The Bloom-writer accepts the sentences that the language imposes on her.

The Bloom-writer has less power than the language, thence the power that her language has.

The tourist-writer has more power than the language, thence the weakness her language has.

Sometimes it is necessary to remember the obvious: if you give strength to something, that thing becomes strong; if you impose your strength on something, that thing becomes weak.

Obesity—There are obese sentences, sentences with a gut.

Every adjective is an obese threat to the sentence. A good example is the previous sentence. There is less obesity in the sentence: every adjective is a threat to the sentence, than in the sentence: every adjective is an obese threat to the sentence.

An obese-word is a word that does not move ahead. A sofa word.

Obsolete—Things do not become obsolete, but the names that are attributed to them do.

Language should not give names to things, but rather names to the movement of things.

What is the velocity of your words? What is the immobility of your words?

Bloom-literature imposes an unforeseeable velocity. Certain works of literature, on the other hand, take on an average velocity. This, then, is what one should avoid.

That which does not become obsolete: untamable speed.

Odd—Every literary text should be odd-numbered, or rather: divided by two, it should not have a remainder of zero. The remainder of a text, that which remains after we read it, will never be zero. If it were zero, if all of its parts were distributed in precise manner, if at the end we look at the text and have the same feeling a mathematician gets after solving a difficult equation, then we have made a mistake on the literary balance sheet, or rather: the process. We have not created literature, we have created a report.

If we arrive at a result, we have not arrived at literature. If we attain literature, we have not attained a result.

P

Pathology—Literature has illnesses just like all other organisms. However, in Bloom-literature, there is an inversion of the concepts of health and illness. If, outside of literature, health is the repetition of a normal state associated with predictability in the behavior of the organism, within literature, this description corresponds with a pathological state. A stable text is ill.

Within literature, pathology is tedium and health is the constant change of the symptoms of the sentence. The first sentence manifests a high fever, the second sentence a red flush in the face, the third sentence irritation of the skin, the fourth sentence an obvious grave illness, and so on and so forth. This, then, is the health of a text: successive pathologies that fight amongst themselves and constantly take each other's places. Illness in Bloom-literature is an illness when it is stable; unstable illnesses reveal the vigorous march forward of the text.

Patience—Patience might possess a substance that is eternal. As for the substances that exist in this world—a glass full of wine, a woman full of desire, and a sentence full of literature—only impatience will be useful with them.

If, by chance, a patient text were to cross paths with a patient reader: leave the two of them there, facing each other, waiting.

Photography—Words should not be tourists. Every sentence that takes photographs of a city or a person loses language and gains a photographic apparatus. A sentence should not be a photograph. Before cameras existed, a sentence could do what cameras do, but now if they do it, they do it worse than a camera does: so why do it?

Describing the physical aspects of a person or a house? Everything that can be photographed should not enter into language.

Placebo—All placebo-sentences become useless over time. Placebo-literature is that which excites the reader for a week. However, literature is something that takes place later on.

Position—A text should not have positions, but rather undetectable hiding places. A position is an obvious visibility, and a literary text should only have hints of visibilities. The only evidence will be its invisibility.

But, of course, complete invisibility makes contact impossible. We'll say that what is recommended are intermediate invisibilities. Or: intermediate visibility.

What should remain hidden, without a visible position? That which is most important.

What should be the visible part? That which leads the reader to do more things.

The text that does more work is the text that makes one work more.

And a character should not have a fixed position. If it does, it isn't a person, but an object. A character doesn't have positions, but rather behaviors that are permanently modified. An *indis*-position is a moment about which we don't know how it will end. And a position isn't even a moment. It is a non-moment. A non-occurrence.

In literature as in war: the position of the text, like that of the enemy, should be a mystery, something that requires investigation.

Prophecy—Prophecy should be uttered at the beginning of a sentence, and its fulfillment should occur at the end of the sentence. Not prophecies made a thousand years in advance. Prophecies made half a sentence in advance.

And the prophecy made in the first half of the sentence should fail. The second half of the sentence is the failure of the inclination of the first part. But to fail here isn't to fail. To fail is to succeed in some other place. The second half of the sentence repeats a prophecy that didn't exist yet. Or rather: it's a surprise.

R

Reality—Bloom-reality is an invention of language, not the other way around. The airplane was invented by the empty space that remained between a few words. Bloom-reality is the thickening of certain letters: the volume of things is the result of wide letters.

Right—A sentence doesn't have right and left sides the way mammals do. A sentence has right and left sides the way a sphere does. And this difference is important and should be pondered.

If the two sides of a sentence are fixed, this means that the sentence is always received from the same point of view. In this case: either the reader is an imbecile or the sentence is an imbecile.

S

Sacrilege—The obviousness of successive sentences. Beauty where there is no blemish. Blemish where there isn't some fleeting beauty. A sentence that appears to end.

Scaffold—A scaffold is an intermediary structure that exists during a process; and it is classically understood that it should disappear at work's end. Of course that is an exaggeration. Or rather: a mistake. What should disappear when the work comes to an end is that which is least interesting. The end is the end, the best is the best.

Scaffolding in literature allows us to ascend and then take action at a determined point that is higher than usual. Without scaffolding, all of literature would be created at a level barely higher than that of reptiles. Without scaffolding, man creates literature at a biped's height, or rather: among all mammals, it is average height. And a bipedal verse or the verse of an average mammal cannot arouse the enthusiasm of more than a generation. Scaffolding is, then, indispensable. Certain texts, like certain birds, float very high above the earth only because at a certain moment, someone offered them the possibility of ascending safely.

But a scaffold can also be transformed into a final structure. If the scaffold were stronger and more efficient than the principal façade of a narrative, then the scaffolding is what should remain.

It's a question of trajectory—action—and of reaching a destination—the end.

Don't look at me when I arrive, look at me while I'm making progress.

Sentence—We can think of a flood that begins at the first letter of the sentence and doesn't end on the last letter of the sentence (because some of the water and the energy will pass over to the next sentence). A sentence cannot be like a cup that contains docile drinking water; a sentence is a cup that tries to hold back a flood. And cannot do so.

Every sentence is an opportunity to inaugurate a world. Bloom-literature takes advantage of this opportunity.

Simultaneous—Nothing happens odd-numbered and singularly. Every thing, even if it is big, is just a part. An elephant, for example, or an enormous building. There are no lives separate from others, lives that go from beginning to end like a chemistry experiment in test tubes. Demonstrating that life is simultaneous is essential. There is no story of a man: Mr. Jonas. Or of a family. There are, rather, men with other men and women, things, plants, the neighbor's dog, and the language that exists in the world and is spoken by anonymous people.

Individual stories are violence to language. Language is an organism that likes angles and unexpected side routes.

The story of a single second across the entire world is more sensible than a story of a man who fell in love with a woman, then another man entered the picture, and . . .

Language is more lateral than longitudinal. It isn't immobile; it moves by immobilizing time, which is different.

Solidifying—Method inimical to Bloom-literature. To solidify is to immobilize.

To the contrary: to melt and to evaporate.

To make all matter ungraspable.

To construct the index of graspability of a sentence, just as there can be an index of graspability of an object (object with a handle/object without a handle, etc).

It is clear that a teacup with a handle can be grasped more easily.

It is also clear that a sentence should not have a handle that allows someone to grasp it with one hand.

Sentences in Bloom-literature do not have handles for the lazy. Either you grasp the sentence with two hands or the sentence falls.

In order to grasp certain objects, you need two hands and all your attention. Thus the Bloom-sentence.

Space—The movement of certain heavenly bodies in space not only influences the seas. The sentence, too.

The sentence and the sea, affected by the moon.

Stalactites—A sentence should have earth below it and sky above: quotidian and elevation. Stalactites are threats of sky above the reader; stalagmites, threats of earth.

Substance—Literature is a substance. You can find it in greater or lesser concentration.

When you look at a text, what you should ask is: What amount of literary substance is there in this sentence? And that one?

There are sentences with a .0002 concentration of literature-substance, and sentences with a .98 concentration of literature. There are even sentences that are completely full, or rather: no trace of anything that isn't literature.

When faced with a Bloom-sentence, one would never say: it's almost all water, and some literature. What one would say is: it's almost all literature and no water.

A Bloom-sentence is insoluble. You can put as much water in there as you want; it will retain its power.

(An imbecilic reader is one whose reading translates the process of spilling water on the sentences.)

Sunday—There is also Sunday language. It is language that does not move forward. It is language that strolls around where it has always strolled and at every turn says: how nice!

Symptoms—Symptoms in a sentence are inclinations revealed by the external part of the words. Because words also have an internal part, and this is not revealed by the symptoms. Symptoms in literature are appearances, let's say: letters. However, sometimes the word is written as *no*, and its internal nucleus is written as *yes*. Other times the symptoms correspond with the nucleus: the word *no* is made up of an internal *no*.

The asymmetry between the symptoms of a work of literature and its nucleus yields the amount of Bloom in that work. The greater the asymmetry, the greater the amount of Bloom-literature.

Syncopation—A text that fears momentary syncopation fears movement, for only matter that moves can come to a stop. Stopping something already at rest is unnecessary.

Of course, syncopation should be seen as the moment that precedes acceleration or deceleration. The moment that precedes a change in direction.

Syncopation in a text—the apparent break or absolute stoppage—is, ultimately, the foothold. The surprising change of direction is preceded by an abrupt stop.

Harmony in a literary text is evidence of movement that is uniform. That is to say: predictable.

Syncopation allows for unpredictability. Harmony despises it.

A predictable literary text is not a literary text. It's a tourist's guidebook.

Synthetic—A sentence must. But also can.

T

Tangent—Any light touch might be brutal. Delicacy is merely one way not to kill. Any Bloom-sentence should trace a tangential line to other sentences. However, this connection will not be narrative.

Technique—Each sentence should have its own technique. A technique that is prolonged over time becomes outdated. The next sentence is the next period of time. If you use the same technique in the next time period, you're running late.

Utilizing one technique per book is the same as wanting to utilize the same second for ten years.

All old time is useless; it should be placed in the trash.

However, technique is not a massacre of the spontaneous. Technique is being aware of the spontaneous.

Technique is not a docile dog, it is an unpredictable animal to which you think you can give commands. If a given technique is a domestic animal, then leave that technique aside. All that is domestic is that which you already know, and the domestic can only yield a 2nd domesticity.

Domestic animals eat the food you give them. Vicious animals fight over food that you don't even recognize.

All sentences that result from a battle, even a short one, are stronger than sentences that result from a contract.

You should only use techniques that make you imperfect, that is: that make you search for different perfections.

All imperfection is a beginning.

Your Words Matter

Your Words Matter

Your Words Matter

www.ingramcontent.com/pod-product-compliance
Lightning Source LLC
Chambersburg PA
CBHW070522010526
44118CB00012B/1054